ONE-MINUTE

Academic Functional Assessment and Interventions

"Can't" Do It ... or "Won't" Do It?

Joe Witt

Ray Beck

05 04 03 02 01 7 6 5 4 3

Edited by Sandra Collier
Cover and Text Layout/Design by Tracy Katzenberger

ISBN #1-57035-205-4

Published and Distributed by

SOPRIS
WEST

4093 Specialty Place • Longmont, CO 80504 • (303) 651-2829
www.sopriswest.com

119MIN/KEN/3-01/1.5M/314

ACKNOWLEDGMENTS

Joe Witt would like to acknowledge and thank those members of the LSU Behavior Intervention Team (BIT) whose work contributed in many ways to the ideas presented here. Team members included Amanda VanDerHeyden, Lynn LaFluer, Gary Duhon, Bruce Mortenson, and co-leader, Dr. George Noell. In particular, Donna Gilbertson of the BIT team was indispensable to this project because she researched and tested many of the interventions presented here.

CONTENTS

INTRODUCTION

One-Minute Functional Assessment

Functional assessment is a process for discovering what can help a child learn at an optimal level. That is, functional assessment is a way to systematically determine "what works" for a particular child using strategies that are readily available to all classroom teachers. Functional assessment is not that different from what good teachers are already doing in their classrooms: trying different strategies, then monitoring student progress to determine if the attempted strategies "work."

The teacher who has discovered that a student is much more successful when he is allowed to respond by *saying* math facts rather than *writing* math facts has used a functional assessment process. So why not just use good instruction with all students and not bother with formal functional assessment? For most students, good instruction is all that is needed. Some students, however, present challenges. A positive outcome of this is that there are so many effective instructional practices that the teacher has to narrow them down to those which might be most effective and practical for a given situation. Otherwise, the teacher is perhaps using precious instructional time on activities that don't work. Our goal is to help teachers be efficient and effective in this process.

In functional assessment, it is assumed that a student's performance in the classroom is affected by two basic things: what happens prior to the student's performance and what happens as a consequence of the student's performance. Put another way, we assume that the learning environment (i.e., teacher, peers, physical environment, etc.) affects the learner. This is a generally recognized and fundamental assumption. However, functional assessment is a method to move beyond generalities into the more specific casual factors of *what*, *who*, *when*, and *under what conditions* the environment has a pronounced effect on student performance.

The effects of the specific environment for a particular student can serve to either enhance performance or detract from it. For example, carefully teaching the child can enhance performance while a pesky peer who talks to the child can detract from it. This process is illustrated in Figure 1 where student performance can be accelerated or decelerated by factors coming either before or after the performance.

Figure 1. Functional Assessment Grid

	Maximize These Activities	Minimize These Activities
Before Performance	Effective Instructional Activities or Other Events	Detractions, Distractions, and Disruptions
After Performance	Effective Feedback or Consequences	Consequences which decrease academic performance (e.g., attention from peers for playing)

In most classrooms the child's performance is preceded by instruction (e.g., a teacher-directed lesson) and is followed by simple teacher feedback (e.g., "You got 22 correct today—that's a great improvement over yesterday!"). Although standard educational methods, such as instruction and feedback, are effective with most students, functional assessment can be used for those students who are not progressing with normal instruction. Functional assessment can also help us to understand how to help a student who is not progressing by understanding the reasons for the lack of progress.

Chapter 1 contains procedures for discovering which of the most common reasons progress is hampered. Chapter 2 provides a review of how to use Precision Teaching, a tool which is essential to the One-Minute Functional Assessment. In Chapter 3, procedures are described for conducting the One-Minute Functional Assessment. Chapters 4-6 describe specific intervention procedures to meet the child's needs.

Compared to other methods of functional assessment, the One-Minute Functional Assessment is more precise and easier, especially for those already using the Precision Teaching model or *Basic Skill Builders*. Those using the Precision Teaching and/or *Basic Skill Builders* are already doing most of the work of functional assessment and this book allows one to use functional assessment to be more successful with the "tough to teach."

CHAPTER 1

How Does Functional Assessment Work?

A story that was going around a few years ago is a good example of functional assessment.

> A convenience store manager was concerned because kids were hanging around the store's parking lot. He wanted to put an end to the loitering and decided he would try increasing the lighting in the parking lot. After doing this, he looked out his window and the *kids were still there*. Next he tried posting signs that said "NO LOITERING." He looked again and the *kids were still there*. He then observed the kids and noticed they enjoyed listening to rock music. Based on that observation, he put up loud speakers and blasted classical music into the parking lot. He looked again and the *kids were all gone*.

This story is a good example of functional assessment. The manager had a way to monitor progress (i.e., looking out the window and counting the kids), he had a way to determine if he was being successful (i.e., seeing if the number of kids in the parking lot declined), and he had several good ideas that had a reasonable chance of improving the situation. He then systematically tested each idea and found "what worked." Figure 2 is a representation of the store manager's initial problem, his different approaches to the problem, and the positive resolution.

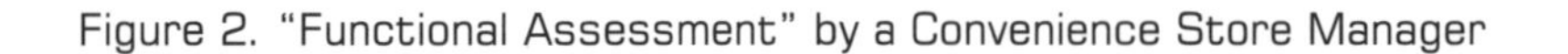

Figure 2. "Functional Assessment" by a Convenience Store Manager

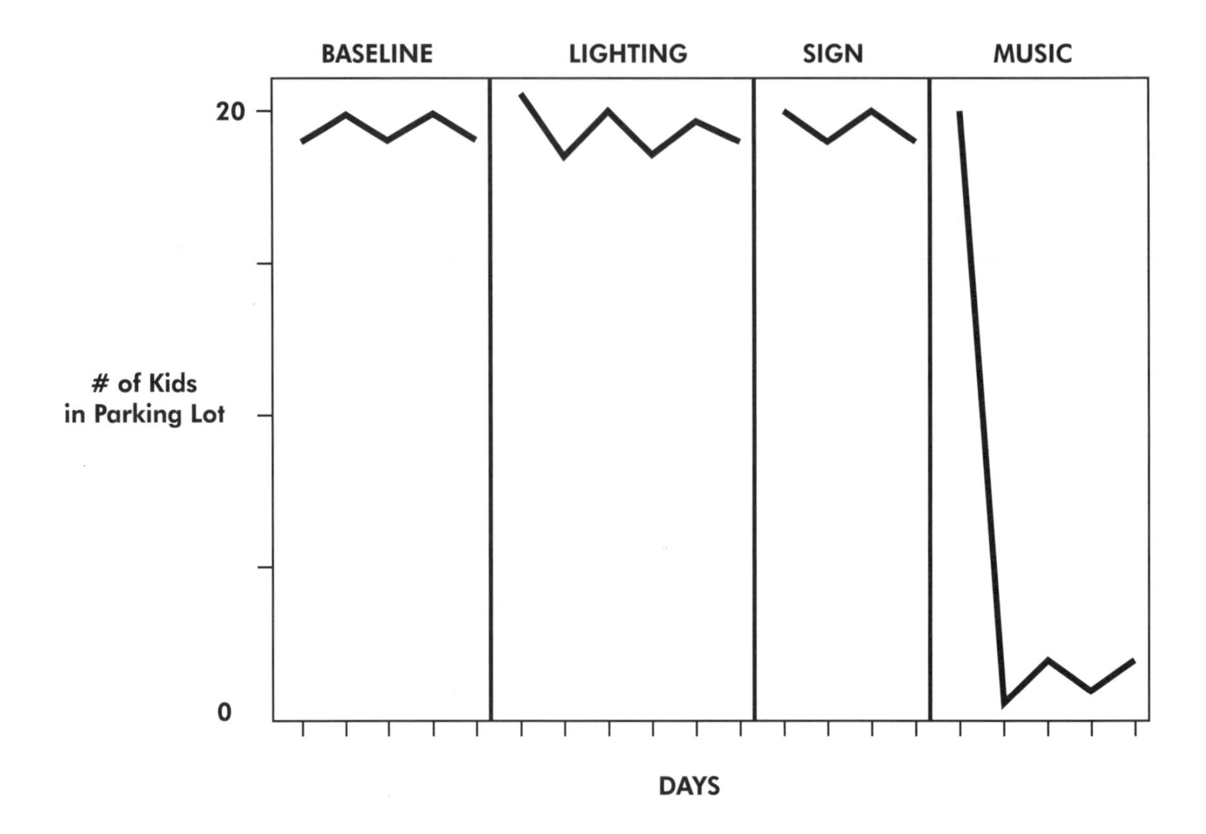

Similarly we can use the functional assessment process to discover how a student learns best. Figure 3 shows one student's progress as her teacher devised and monitored different teaching strategies. Ms. Barton's class was learning the names of each state in the U.S. Most students in the class were performing well using an instruction method which involved pairing up with a peer and taking turns using flash cards. Ms. Barton was concerned with Natasha's lack of progress in this activity. The first modification from the standard instruction for Natasha tried by Ms. Barton was that during the test she would allow Natasha to say the names of the states to her (i.e., See/Say) rather than write the state names (i.e., See/Write).

Figure 3. Results from Ms. Barton

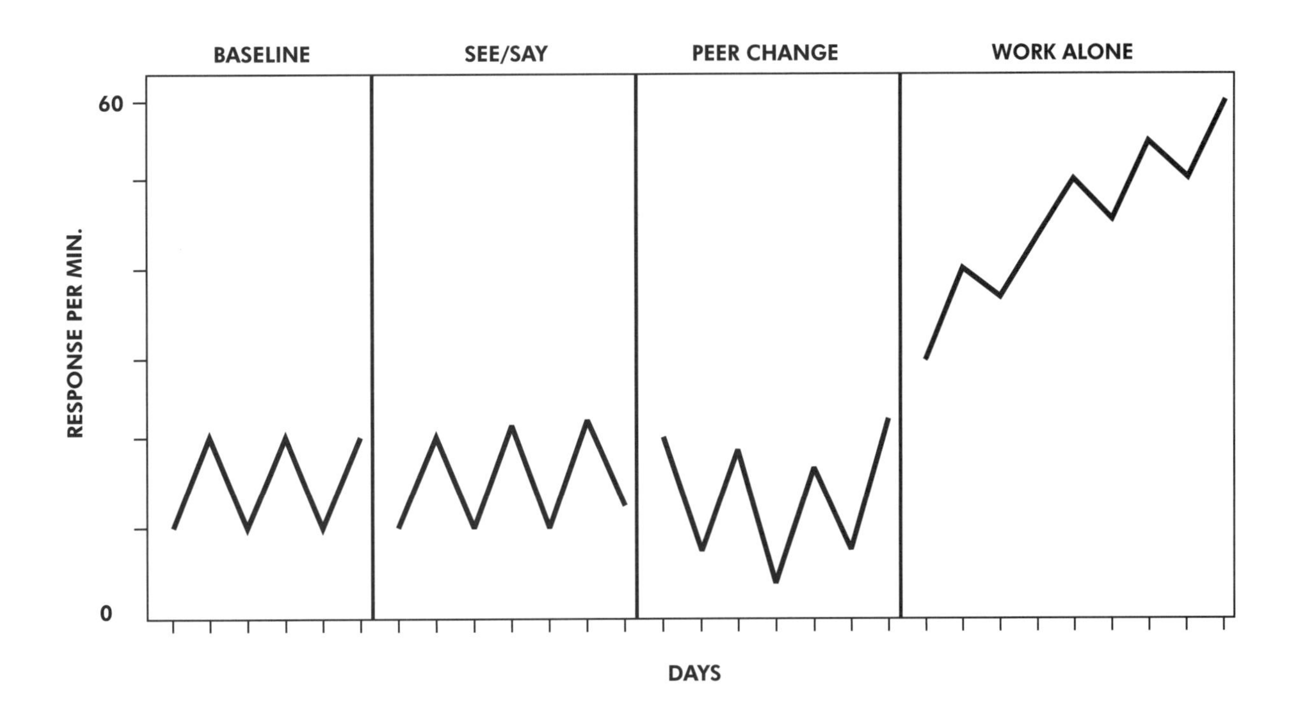

Changing the learning channel for Natasha had no effect. Ms. Barton then noticed that Natasha was talking a lot to her partner instead of practicing with the flash cards. When Ms. Barton changed Natasha's peer, Natasha's performance was unaffected but her new partner's performance decreased. Ms. Barton decided to have Natasha practice by herself so at least she did not interfere with the work of others. Natasha's performance increased dramatically! For Natasha, working alone was the key.

The teacher in the example used all three tools of functional assessment: (a) a daily measure of knowledge of states, (b) a way to determine progress, and (c) some good ideas about how to improve performance.

Functional assessment then requires a familiarity with factors *under the teacher's control* that influence learning. We will be most interested in two categories of occurrences in the classroom which enhance or detract from student performance: those that the student experiences *before* performance and those which occur immediately *after* performance. Other factors such as the student's intelligence, learning abilities, and neurological functioning are not under the control of the teacher and, therefore, are not a major focus of functional assessment.

The Key Elements of Functional Assessment

Functional assessment is a process which has a long history and tradition. Although it is becoming increasingly popular, it is important to be aware that functional assessment is based upon sound fundamentals in the science of learning, assessment, and instruction. In this regard, functional assessment shares several key elements with the Precision Teaching model including:

- Fluency Standards and Aims,
- One-Minute Skill Sheets,
- Rate of Student Responding as the Basic Unit of Measurement,
- Continuous Progress Monitoring and Decision Making, and
- The Standard Celeration Chart.

To these, we would add the following key elements that are important for conducting the One-Minute Functional Assessment and the evaluation of instructionally relevant variables.

- **Assessment must consider factors that are functional.** Functional factors differ from structural factors, such as intelligence, motivation, and other things that reside within the student, and are therefore not under the direct control of the teacher. Do factors such as learning disabilities affect student performance? Of course they do, but they are beyond the teacher's control in the classroom.

  The word "functional" within the phrase "functional assessment" means that the focus is on factors in the student's environment which are under teacher control and which make a difference in student performance. The word "functional" is shorthand for "functional relationship" which is a scientific term for changes in a particular behavior, such as student math performance, that occur only when a particular condition is present.

For example, Johnny talks a lot in class. However, it is noticed that the only time Johnny talks excessively is when he is sitting next to Jimmy. In other words, there seems to be a correlation between Johnny talking and his sitting next to Jimmy. There may be a relationship, but it may not be a *functional* relationship. To discover whether it is a functional relationship, we have to perform a quick test. The test involves having Jimmy sit next to Johnny for ten minutes during math and for ten minutes during reading. The rest of the time, Johnny sits alone. If Johnny's talking only occurs when Jimmy is near, then we are pretty sure there is a correlation between the environment (i.e., sitting next to Jimmy) and a particular behavior (i.e., Johnny's talking). In other words, Johnny's talking is a *function of* sitting next to Jimmy.

- **Evaluating individual student progress is preferable to comparing the student with other students.** Typical tests provide information about whether one student is performing better or worse than other students. This does not help very much when designing instruction except to say that *something* needs to be done about a low-performing student. In functional assessment, we compare a student's performance using one type of instruction with the same student's performance when using a different instructional strategy. If the student performs better with one strategy than another, then this tells us to use the better strategy with the student. Hence, we know what to do to help the student.

- **Testing is linked to instruction.** A related issue is that by testing different strategies with a student, the outcome is the identification of an instructional practice or practices which improve responding. These practices *are* the intervention. Standardized tests, on the other hand, provide no guidance about which particular strategies to use.

- **Change one thing at a time.** To isolate true functional relations, the classroom detective will want to change only one thing at a time. This will simplify instruction; however, it does take more time for assessment. For example, to improve the performance of a student we could change our instructional approach *and* add positive consequences at the same time. However, if the student improves, we don't know whether it was due to the instruction, the positive consequences, or a combination of the two. It would be better to do things in an orderly sequence where first we increase instruction, then we discontinue instruction and add positive consequences. If we only evaluated both factors and they were effective, then we might use both things with the student when only one was necessary. Proceeding sequentially can take a little longer, but it is more accurate.

- **Daily measurement of the skill—an additional note.** *Basic Skill Builders* sheets (available from Sopris West, Longmont, CO) provide a dependable, sensitive, stable, and repeatable measure of performance. Teaching and learning occur *daily*. Student achievement is very sensitive to the learning environment created by the teacher. To evaluate the effects of different teaching procedures, it is important to monitor student performance on a daily basis. Standardized tests are not useful for this purpose because they cannot be administered daily, and they are not sensitive to small but significant changes in a single skill. Presenting a different task each day, as might be done with curriculum-based assessment or informal assessment procedures, can pose difficulty because changes in the student's performance each day could be due to the task being easier or more difficult from day to day rather than the instruction method. *Basic Skill Builders* sheets can be used daily, they can be administered repeatedly, and they are carefully sequenced to allow for continuous assessment as the student becomes more proficient.

Basic Skill Builders sheets provide a means for monitoring the true progress of students. It can be said with confidence that a student who consistently responds correctly to more questions each day is learning. The rule is that three days of flat data or less than 25% growth per week means the student's rate of skill acquisition is such that the instructional strategy should be changed. With functional assessment, we will use a similar process to quickly and efficiently find antecedents and consequences which promote student mastery.

CHAPTER 2

Precision Teaching Overview

Background

For the teacher or parent unfamiliar with Precision Teaching, two concepts guide the procedure. The first follows the belief that in order for students to remember, transfer, and generalize a skill across settings, they must be "fluent." That is, they must not only demonstrate accuracy with the skill, but they must display speed as well. When students are fluent (accuracy plus speed) they can recall the skill with less effort, transfer the skill to more complex tasks, and eventually generalize the skill across different settings automatically, with confidence and comfort.

A third grade teacher recently reported that as her students practiced words from a new reading list at 80 words per minute (wpm), those same words seemed easier when placed in short phrases. The short phrases were practiced until the students reached an aim of 120 wpm. The teacher then challenged the students to read orally at 180 wpm in passage format.

The interesting thing about this scenario is that from the original word list practiced to fluency (80 wpm) to reading passages aloud (180 wpm), the same words began appearing in the students' creative writing stories. The teacher discovered that as new words were practiced to fluency levels in one setting (reading), the more readily the new words became available to the students in another setting (creative writing). It appeared that as students developed a sense of fluency and comfort in one task, they found it easier and less burdensome to use the skill in a higher level task.

To help students reach fluency, teachers either develop their own skill sheets, use district curriculum, or refer to a series of over 1,500 skill sheets that have been developed in a number of core skills such as math, reading, spelling, handwriting, and grammar (Sopris West). In requiring both speed and accuracy, the teacher sets high expectations, slices the curriculum into small parts, and asks the students to practice the skill through one-minute timings. The student who becomes fluent in basic math computation will remember that 4 x 3 is 12 during practice and will apply the skill to story problems.

The second important concept to the Precision Teaching model centers around the need for a standardized system of monitoring, displaying, and making decisions about student performance. The measurement idea promoted here not only helps teachers develop and use a common language regarding student performance, but also demonstrates how to visually display the data and apply a set of rules for better decision making.

The Precision Teaching model, which includes the Standard Celeration Chart, was developed by Ogden R. Lindsley, University of Kansas, in the mid sixties. The "chart" can graphically display responses that occur as infrequently as once in a 24-hour period to as high as 1,000 times per minute. Student progress can be monitored for up to 20 weeks on one sheet of 8½" x ll" piece of paper (see Figure 4). This method of charting incorporates a semilogarithmic scale with "Count Per Minute" on the vertical axis and "Days" across the horizontal axis. Using a form of a semilogarithmic scale helps to standardize our measurement system that when visually displayed across days, weeks, and months could be easily interpreted by teachers, students, parents, administrators, and support staff.

Figure 4. Standard Celeration Chart

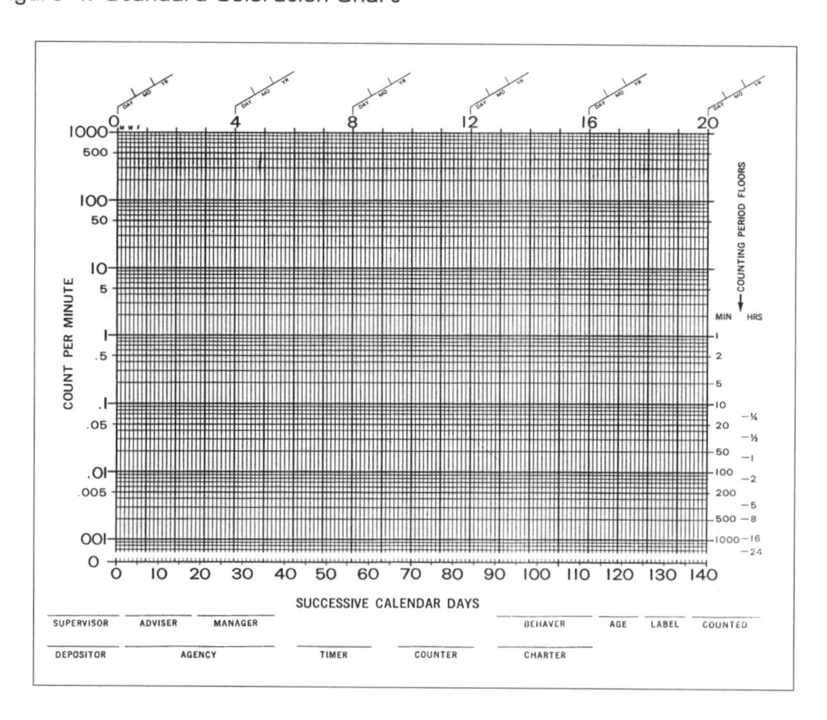

At first glance, the chart may seem too technical, however, with some practice, teachers and students alike can convert a series of 20 raw scores to 20 "dots" in less than a minute. While a copy is available in the appendix, the use of this chart will be explained later in this chapter.

We, therefore, think that the element of fluency coupled with a standard measurement system can not only provide teachers with a set of procedures that help students learn and maintain core skills but can also greatly assist in implementing a functional assessment procedure that leads to better instructional and curricular decisions.

Elements of Precision Teaching

Several philosophical underpinnings guide the Precision Teaching model. First, teachers and parents must believe in setting high expectations for *all* students, including those with disabilities, those identified for Title I services, those placed in remedial settings, or those spending the entire day in a general education classroom. *All* means *all*. Second, teachers and parents must believe in the value of sequencing the curriculum, allowing one skill to build upon another. Accompanying this hierarchical order of building skills, users of this philosophy must resurrect the almost forgotten principle of practice and overlearning where students, through the use of one-minute timings, practice, practice, and practice the skill to a predetermined level of fluency. Finally, teachers must believe in monitoring student performance directly and continuously and in using the data gathered to make instructional and curricular decisions.

Four Steps in Using Precision Teaching

Step 1. Selecting the Skill

Selecting a specific skill for practice requires an answer to several questions.

a. Is the student fluent in the basic skill and tool skill? The first step is to determine if the student is already fluent in the skill. To do this, the teacher selects a Skill Sheet or task that is best aligned with the teaching objective and/or one that best represents the student's instructional level. If after several one-minute practice sessions a student does not appear fluent (accuracy plus speed) or is not progressing toward fluency, the teacher needs to determine whether the student has the "tool skill" necessary for the "basic skill." For example, in Precision Teaching language, tool skills are those skills that either precede or accompany the basic skill. In the case of single-column addition, "writing numbers" might be considered the tool skill necessary to the basic skill of addition.

Speaking of tool skills, there is an interesting story about musician Ray Charles. After 50 years of playing the piano, he was asked during a recent radio interview, "Do you still practice a lot?" His response to the interviewer was, "I try to practice every day. I practice things like scales and chords and movements of my hands ... you gotta practice." His point being that the tool skills of playing scales and chords, accompanied by hand-movements, are essential to the basic skill of composing and performing music.

Many students with basic skill deficits (e.g., math, reading, and spelling) also have tool skill deficits that prohibit progress in building fluency in the basic skill. For example, in penmanship, circles and slashes are the tool skills that when put together eventually make up manuscript and cursive letters. Circles and slashes someday make up individual numbers as well. Some students who have difficulty with math computation also have difficulty with the tool skill of writing numbers. A teacher who has an expectation of 45 correct digits per minute in simple addition facts might discover that Tommy can only write numbers at 30 per minute. Writing numbers then becomes the tool skill necessary for Tommy to reach fluency in the basic skill of 45 correct digits per minute in math computation. This type of tool skill deficit also might involve a student who is expected to hear and then write spelling words at 12 words per minute. If she cannot write letters at 75-100 per minute, there is good chance that the tool skill of writing letters will impede, if not prohibit, the basic skill of spelling. The ability to "say sounds" and to associate sounds and letters is the tool skill necessary for and directly correlated to the skill of reading words orally at 200 correct per minute.

b. What Learning Channel is most common to this skill? Let us assume for the moment that a student does not have a tool skill deficit and the teacher has a set of fluency objectives for him in reading, math, handwriting, spelling, grammar, and dictionary skills. The next step is to include a Learning Channel statement. Here a simple system of Input and Output (see Figure 5) is used where the student is viewed as receiving information through the ears or eyes (either hears it or sees it), and then demonstrates the skill through his mouth or hands (either says it or writes it). Using the Think/Write Channel, a student might "think" and "write" all combinations of numbers in one minute that equal 12 (e.g., 4×3, 7+5, 6+6, 16–4, etc.).

Figure 5. Learning Channels

In the case of oral reading, the student receives and decodes a word using the See Channel and expresses the word through the Say Channel. Another way of putting it is See to Say or See/Say words. With math facts, the student typically sees the problem on the worksheet and then writes the answer (See/Write math facts). During the exercise of spelling, the student hears the word and writes the answer (Hear/Write spelling words). Table 1 offers a more complete view of the Learning Channel Matrix.

Table 1. Learning Channel Matrix

INPUT	OUTPUT
See	Write
Hear	Say
Think	Mark
Point	Touch
Touch	Do

c. What Skill Sheet best represents this skill? The next task is to select an appropriate Skill Sheet so the student can demonstrate the extent to which she can or cannot meet the teacher's objective. As we mentioned earlier, teachers either develop skill sheets, use existing curriculum, or use individual sheets from the bank of over 1,500 one-minute Skill Sheets in math computation, story problems, fractions, decimals, reading, grammar (language arts), handwriting, map skills, telling time, etc. For topics not available, teachers can easily make their own by following the format presented in existing Skill Sheets. A complete listing of the *Basic Skill Builders* Skill Sheet bank is provided in the Appendix.

d. What is the "Aim"? The fourth requirement in selecting a skill for practice is determining an Aim or expectation that, when reached and maintained, helps the student remember the skill over time, transfer the skill to a more complex skill, and generalize the skill across settings. Aims are determined in several ways. The first is to use a set of standards established by the *Great Falls, Montana, Sacajawea Plan*, where hundreds of students helped generate a set of frequency ranges that can be used as a guide for most academic skills. A second way is to use *several students* who are considered fluent in a specific skill. In this case the teacher uses the group average or median frequencies over three trials. Some teachers establish Aims by taking the one-minute exercise themselves and then reducing their scores by about one-third. The last, and perhaps the most defensible, is to use real world frequencies; that is, those frequencies commonly accepted as standard in academics or in the world-of-work.

Table 2. Suggested Aims From Great Falls, Sacajawea Plan

	Per Minute
Reading:	
See/Say Sounds	60-80
See/Say Letters	80-100
See/Say Words Isolation	80-100
See/Say Words Passage	200+
Math:	
See/Write Numbers Random	100+
Think/Write Numbers Serial	120+
See/Write Math Facts	70+
Spelling:	
Hear/Write Words (letters)	80-100
Hear/Write Words	15+
Handwriting:	
Think/Write Slashes	200+
Think/Write Circles	100+
Think/Write Letters Manuscript	75+
Think/Write Letters Cursive	125+

Step 2. Practicing the Skill

Independent practice should be considered *after* the concept has been taught. Only after teaching, modeling, and guided practices will independent practice have any positive effect. It will do little good for Tommy to practice 3 x 4, unless he has first been taught multiplication tables (e.g., 3 x 4 = 12). There are obvious exceptions where students have self-taught. Again, in this case, if the student is fluent, she has undoubtedly practiced the skill independently.

Sam Snead, considered one of the best golfers in the game, finished first in 185 tournaments, including the Masters, three PGA Championships, and one British Open. When asked about his athletic prowess, he responded, "I practiced as much as anyone .... For years I hit 500 balls a day ... There is no such thing as natural talent, there is natural ability, but talent comes only after relentless practice and fine-tuning."

Practice as used in the Precision Teaching exercises is viewed as a support procedure to the curriculum, where the student, through multiple opportunities to respond, will have a better chance of embedding the skill. The idea of practice has a long and well-rooted history in athletics, music, the arts, writing, and, yes, basic skills. In fact, practice for generations of learners was an essential ingredient to instruction. We continue to support the argument that any person who is considered proficient in any skill has undoubtedly practiced that skill over and over and over.

If students are to be considered fluent, then practice and overlearning is fundamental. Adding to this, if the skill is to be maintained, transferred, and generalized over time, the student must practice the skill at higher rates than what the real world may require. Students need to have their basic skills immediately available so that they may be transferred across environments.

In trying to make practice something more than long exercises of laborious drill, one-minute timings were introduced. One-minute timings are not only a manageable unit of measurement for academic behaviors, they are fun for the students to do. One-minute timings also promote self-competitiveness as the students attempt to better their scores from one timing to another. The most important component, however, is that practice must be done daily and with specific performance Aims (fluency statements).

From the menu of Precision Teaching skill sheets that are available in math, reading, language arts, handwriting, map skills, etc., teachers can program for almost any student experiencing a basic skill deficit. From tool skills (e.g., writing numbers) in math to complicated story problems, a nearly complete sequence is available in the *Basic Skill Builders* Skill Sheets Bank. Of help to both students and teachers are the answers that are provided on the reverse side of each Skill Sheet. This allows for immediate feedback and reinforcement. Figure 6 provides a few examples of Basic Skill Sheets. Other examples of skill sheets, including a blank, are available in the appendix.

Figure 6: Samples of *Basic Skill Builders* Sheets

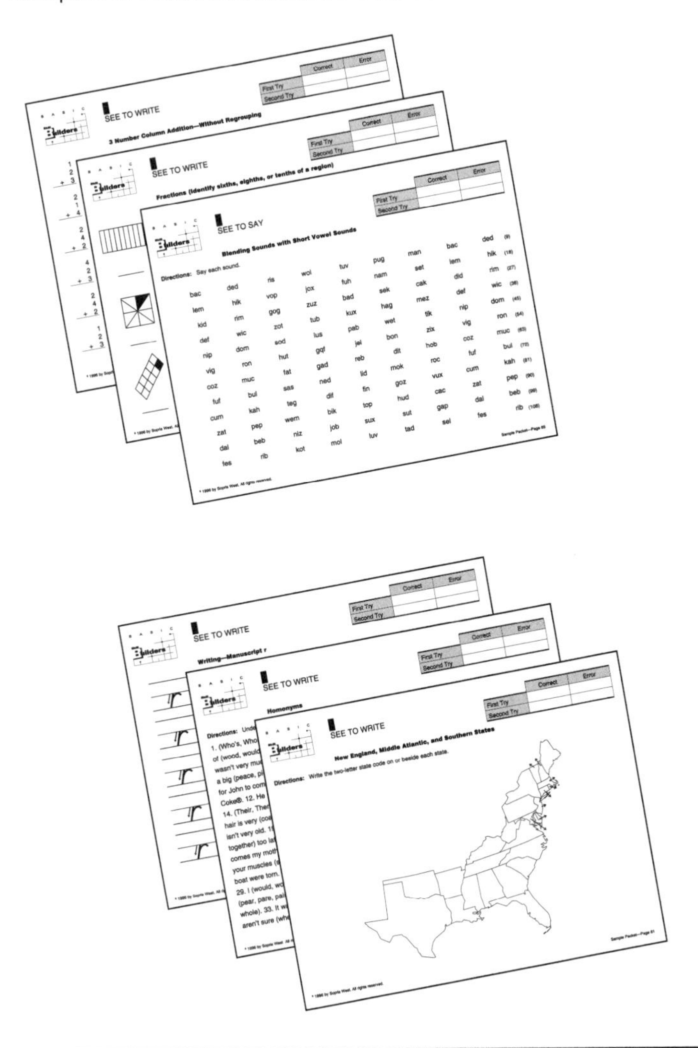

Each student receives a student-folder, a plastic-tip pen, and a small sponge. A selection (four to six) of Skill Sheets is typically housed within the folder. Students place the Skill Sheet of choice under the clear mylar (acetate) taped inside the folder, and when signaled, begin a one-minute timed exercise using the pen. After the timing, students quickly flip the Skill Sheets to the answer sides and score their responses. They can then clean the clear mylar with the dampened sponge and prepare for a second try (see Figure 7).

Figure 7. Student Folder and Materials

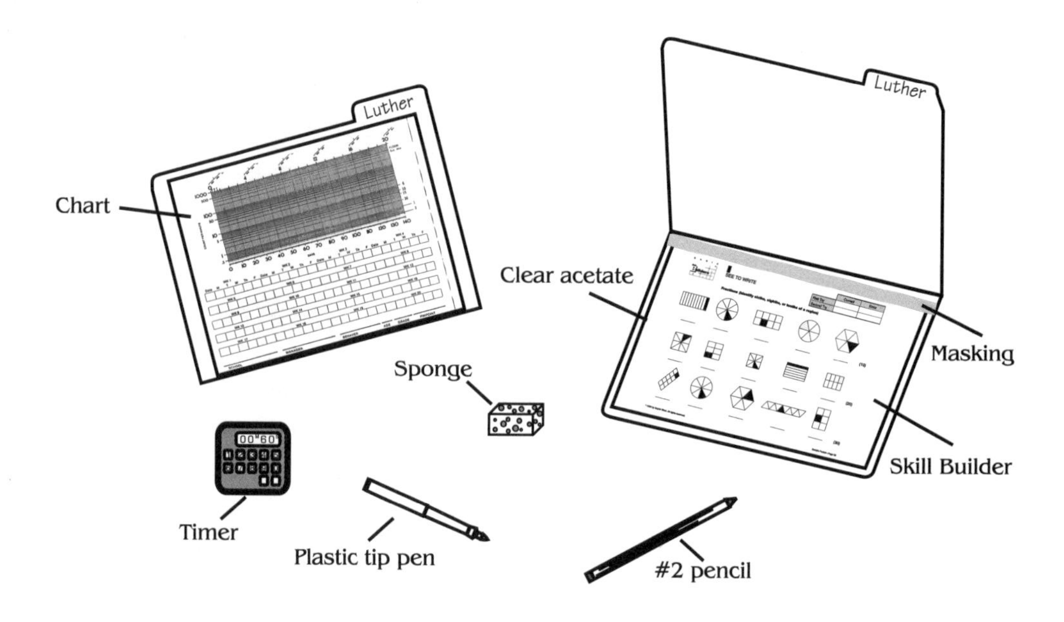

One final word on practice. From the professional literature at least one finding bears repeating—the more a student is academically engaged (time-on-task), the greater chance for academic growth. Academic engagement is perhaps the most predictive event in both ensuring academic progress and preventing behavior problems. Practicing a skill over and over to reach a level of fluency is arguably one of the best ways to keep a student academically engaged.

 3. Monitoring the Skill

The Effective Schools literature consistently makes the case that monitoring student performance is a necessary ingredient in classrooms considered to be effective (Northwest Regional Lab Study, 1995). The argument was made earlier that monitoring student performance and decision making is the counterpart to the need for students to be "fluent."

There are five requirements in monitoring student progress.

a. **Be direct.** The measurement should be taken directly from and reflect the student's current curriculum and/or classroom objective. Unlike indirect measures that are often found in standardized tests, the Precision Teaching approach requires that the measurement be directly aligned with the instruction and/or the curriculum. For example, if a student is studying the 50 states and their geographical/physical locations, the measurement should reflect how well (accuracy plus speed) the student matches the names of states with their precise location on the map. A second illustration might involve a student who is required to read from a specific third-grade passage. Again, the measurement (See/Say words per minute) should be taken directly from the same third-grade passage, as opposed to a standardized test.

a. **Be daily.** Frequent measures are essential to good instructional and curricular decisions and are also necessary for feedback to the student. The Effective Schools literature reports that the more frequently we monitor student performance, the more likely we are to make better decisions and the more likely the student is to show progress. This being the case, measurement should be done every day, and if not every day, as often as possible. In Precision Teaching an effort is made to monitor students on a daily basis. The one-minute timings fit nicely into this model.

c. **Use rate-of-response measurement.** The most sensitive metric in measuring a student's academic performance is rate-of-response, sometimes referred to as frequency. It has the advantage over traditional percent-only methods in that the equation considers count as well as time. For example, when a teacher reports that a student scored 80% correct in a number writing exercise, we don't know whether the task was completed in one minute, one hour, or one day. Rate, on the other hand, has a built-in statement which includes "frequency" (e.g., 45 correct) and time (one minute). Rate, as a formula, is the number of responses divided by time (e.g., $\frac{\text{45 correct}}{\text{1 minute}}$ = 45/minute).

d. **Be displayed using a standard format.** The difficulties in using different graphing formats are (a) the lack of a standard metric, and (b) the confusion in interpreting and deciding what to do next. One teacher, for example, might choose a ¼″ graph, another ½″ , and another a 1″ graph. When teachers use different units of measurement on the axis (vertical/horizontal), the data are sometimes misleading. After charting dozens of students across several academic subjects, the graphs can take on different characteristics and then are difficult to interpret in a consistent and meaningful manner.

Below are two examples of how two sets of data might be confusing. In the first set (Figure 8), the scores of Carla and Richard appear different. It seems that Carla has a steeper rate (slope) of learning than Richard. A closer examination of the same set of data (Figure 9), however, reveals they have exactly the same rate (slope) of learning. In Figure 8, different interval settings were used on the vertical and horizontal axis, while in Figure 9, a modification of the Standard Celeration Chart, the two axes remained standardized.

Figure 8. Equal Interval Graph

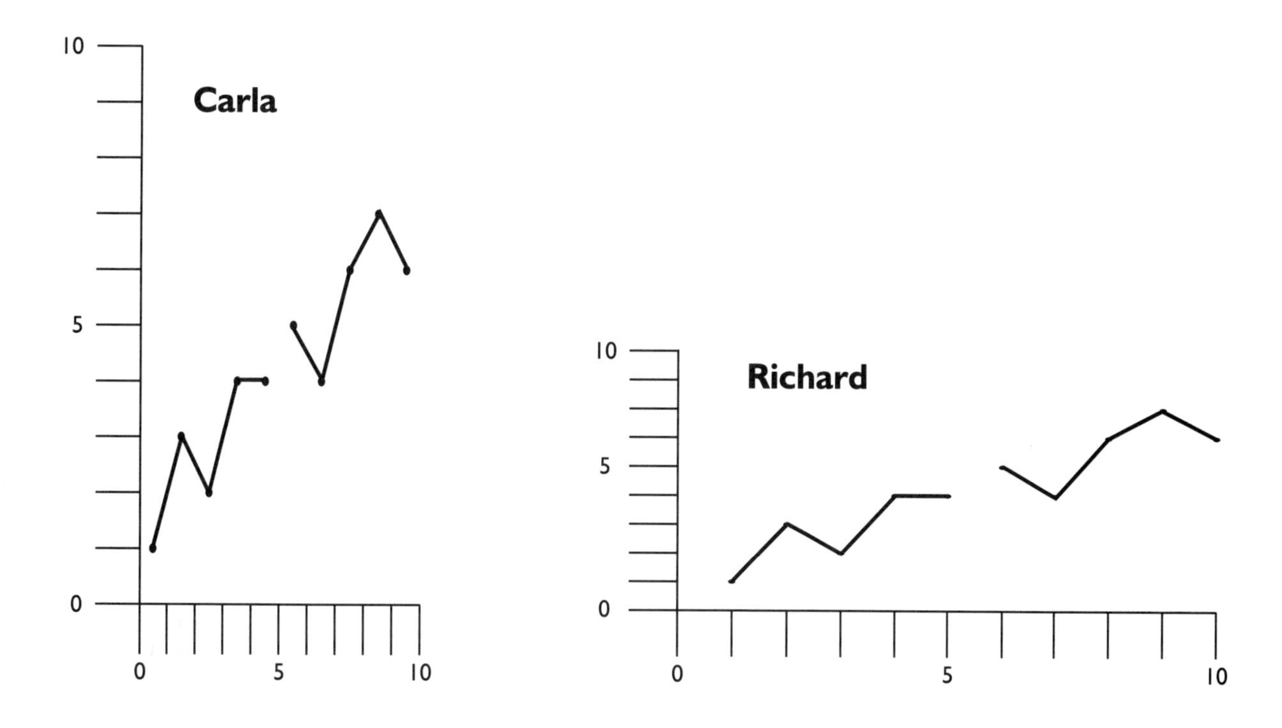

Figure 9: 3-Cycle Academic Chart

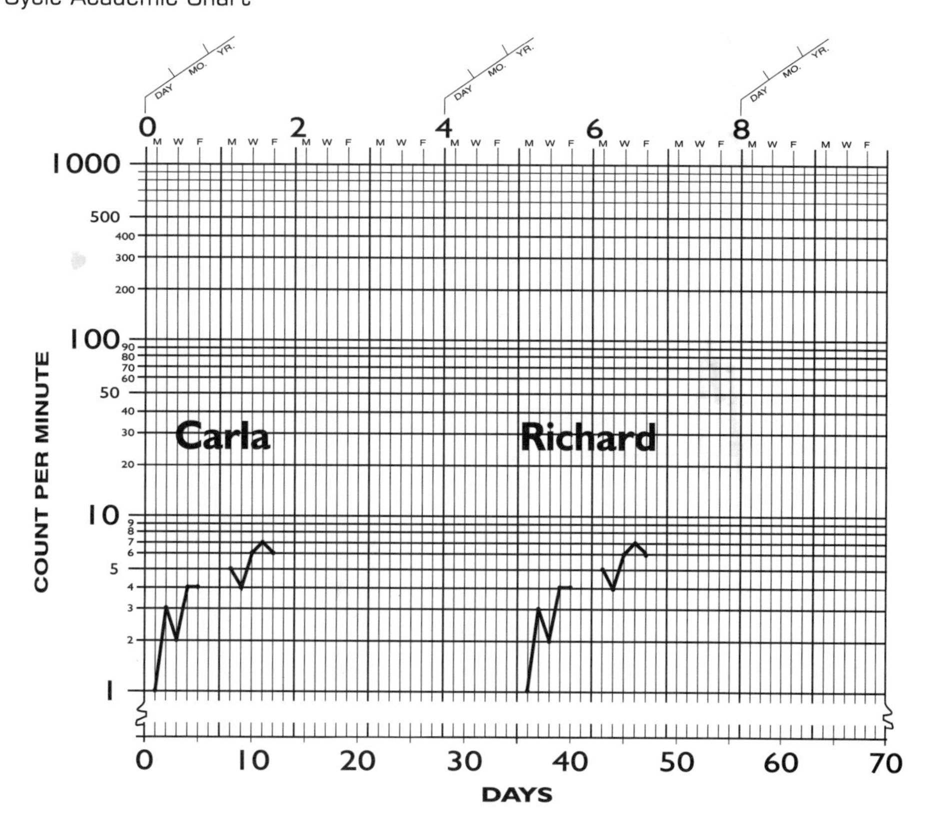

By using the top half of the Standard Celeration Chart developed by Lindsley, the 3-Cycle Academic Chart, teachers and other practitioners are provided a consistent and standardized method of recording and displaying performance, therefore avoiding any misinterpretation or misrepresentation of the data. See the Appendix for a copy of the 3-Cycle Academic Chart.

e. **Use decision-making rules.** The final step is to incorporate a set of guidelines that help teachers adjust their instruction and/or curriculum. The next section helps to clarify.

Step 4. Deciding

Decide if and when to change the *antecedent event* by considering the

- Skill Sheet,
- Learning Channel,
- Aim,
- Instructional procedure, and
- Other environmental conditions.

Decide if and when to change the *consequence* by considering whether to

- reward,
- ignore, or
- punish.

Decision Rules: There are many reasons for monitoring student performance, but none are more important than using the data to make better decisions regarding the appropriateness of the instruction and curriculum being offered the students. To merely "drop dots" on a chart is to waste the time and effort of all concerned. Monitoring a student's performance (past and present) should be done with the intent of assessing where she has been, where she is, and how to predict her future.

To help accomplish this, two simple decision rules, which have evolved from earlier precision teaching work, are incorporated into the model.

If	Then Consider
1. At Aim for two out of three trials	Moving to a more difficult task
2. Three days of little or no growth	Slicing back to easier Skill Sheet
	Adding tool skill practice
	Changing Learning Channel
	Changing the Skill Sheet format
	Including incentive plan
	Instruct to errors

In a later chapter, teachers are shown how to use these guidelines and are given some suggestions on determining whether it's a *Can't Do* or *Won't Do* problem. In addition, antecedent events and consequences will be reviewed, showing how these two conditions affect behavior (academic performance).

Dropping the Dots. . .

Scoring

A well-known principle of learning suggests that the more immediate the feedback (corrects and errors) to the student, the more likely a change in performance. In Precision Teaching, this feedback is provided by immediately scoring and recording the number of corrects and errors.

Following the one-minute exercise, the student in most cases self-corrects by locating the answers on the flip side of the Skill Sheet. In the case of See/Write Addition Facts: Sums to 18, not only are the answers provided, but cumulative scores (digits) are shown in parenthesis at the end of each row. For example, in Figure 10 the student completed three rows and attempted another four problems in the fourth row. His score for this timing would be 50 correct and no errors.

Figure 10. Math Facts Skill Sheet

SEE TO WRITE

	Correct	Error
First Try	50	0
Second Try		

Math Facts: Addition, Subtraction, Multiplication, and Division

6 − 5 = 1	3)18 = 6	6 − 3 = 3	2)12 = 6	9 x 5 = 45	4 x 4 = 16	4 − 4 = 0	6 + 8 = 14	9 − 1 = 8	9 x 3 = 27	8 + 8 = 16	(16)
6 x 1 = 6	9 + 2 = 11	8 x 8 = 64	6 − 6 = 0	4 + 0 = 4	9 x 3 = 27	2 − 1 = 1	7)63 = 9	2)8 = 4	8)64 = 8	5 + 9 = 14	(31)
7 − 2 = 5	6 x 3 = 18	7)49 = 7	8 − 3 = 5	6 + 4 = 10	4 − 2 = 2	4 x 4 = 16	4)36 = 9	7 + 0 = 7	4)16 = 4	3 + 1 = 4	(45)
9)27 = 3	6 x 3 = 18	8)32 = 4	1 x 8 = 8	6 + 0	16 + 2	6 x 1	6 x 6	6 + 8	3 + 7	8 + 8	(62)
9)63	8 − 2	8 x 9	7)56	2 + 2	7 x 6	6 x 8	9 x 5	6 x 4	1)3	6 − 5	(78)
9 x 5	10 + 6	8)56	10 − 8	8 + 9	7)42	6 x 7	11 − 6	6 + 5	12 − 9	9)36	(94)
6 − 3	3 x 3	10 − 5	2)6	4 x 2	7)49	3)21	6 x 3	16 + 3	12 − 4	9)81	(107)

Similar scoring procedures are used with other Skill Sheets, such as grammar exercises, word lists, passages, telling time, story problems, etc. Typically, problems are presented left to right with the total (cumulative) digits in the answers at the end of each row. One exception would be found in "spelling" (Hear/Write words). For example, if the word "beautiful" was spelled "beatiful," the student would secure a score of 8 correct letters in sequence and 1 error. The rationale for this type of scoring is that if the student is given credit for attempting a word that she normally would have avoided, it builds and reinforces "attempts."

Recording

This step requires transferring the score(s) as raw data from the Skill Sheet to a matrix of single boxes that represent specific dates. Figure 11 shows how data from the Skill Sheet are transferred to the set of boxes. Using a slash mark through each box, corrects are entered on the top half while errors are recorded on the bottom half.

Figure 11. Raw Data

	WK 1						WK 2						WK 3				
Date	M	T	W	Th	F	Date	M	T	W	Th	F	Date	M	T	W	Th	F
5/12	50/0	53/1	59/0	65/1	72/0	5/19	68/2	75/1	80/1	82/0	85/1						

	WK 4						WK 5						WK 6				
Date	M	T	W	Th	F	Date	M	T	W	Th	F	Date	M	T	W	Th	F

	WK 7						WK 8						WK 9				
Date	M	T	W	Th	F	Date	M	T	W	Th	F	Date	M	T	W	Th	F

	WK 10				
Date	M	T	W	Th	F

SCHOOL	TEACHER	STUDENT	AGE	GRADE	SKILL
Sanborn	J. Horsfall	Gary	10	5th	Math

Charting

Although a variety of charting methods (e.g., equal interval graphs) are used routinely by teachers, the 3-Cycle Academic Chart is the procedure we recommend. Whatever format is used, however, it is important that the visual display of student performance be presented in a consistent and standard manner. Practitioners using the graphs must be able to easily interpret the information for decision making.

Teachers who choose the Standard Celeration Chart (semilogarithmic) format also have the option of plotting data on a modified 3-Cycle Academic Chart. The advantage of this chart is that most academic behavior occurs between 1 and 300 counts per minute, which permits a visual display of dots on the upper half, while still maintaining a record of the raw scores on the lower half.

At first, charting using the semilogarithmic scale might seem somewhat overwhelming; however, third graders and, on some occasions, even younger children have demonstrated charting competencies. Here are a few simple guidelines to remember when charting.

1. Viewing Figure 12, the vertical lines are "day lines." The lighter lines represent Monday through Saturday, while the heavier lines represent Sunday. In the classroom, the typical "day lines" are Monday through Friday.

2. The horizontal lines are "rate" lines and are interpreted as the number of responses or the count per minute.

3. Student performance can be monitored for 10 weeks which is about one-quarter of the school year.

4. The very bottom of the 3-Cycle Academic Chart provides for the student's name, grade level, skill (pinpoint), age, teacher's name, and school.

5. Starting at the 1-per-minute line, the count is by 1s (e.g., 1/min, 2/min, 3/min, etc.) to the 10-per-minute line, where, because of the logarithmic feature, the count is by 10s (e.g., 10/min, 20/min, 30/min, etc.) to the 100-per-minute line where the count is by 100s (e.g., 100/min, 200/min, 300/min, etc.). Most academic behavior counts range between the 10/min and 300/min lines.

6. Other charting guidelines include: (see Figure 12).

   • = (dot) for correct response

   x = error

   A = Aim—with the apex indicating the Aim-date and the crossbar indicating the Aim-rate

   ⌈ = phase change—depicts the current instructional, curriculum, or environmental arrangement (e.g., skill, Learning Channel, Skill Sheet, other Antecedent Events and/or Consequences)

Figure 12. 3-Cycle Academic Chart Guidelines

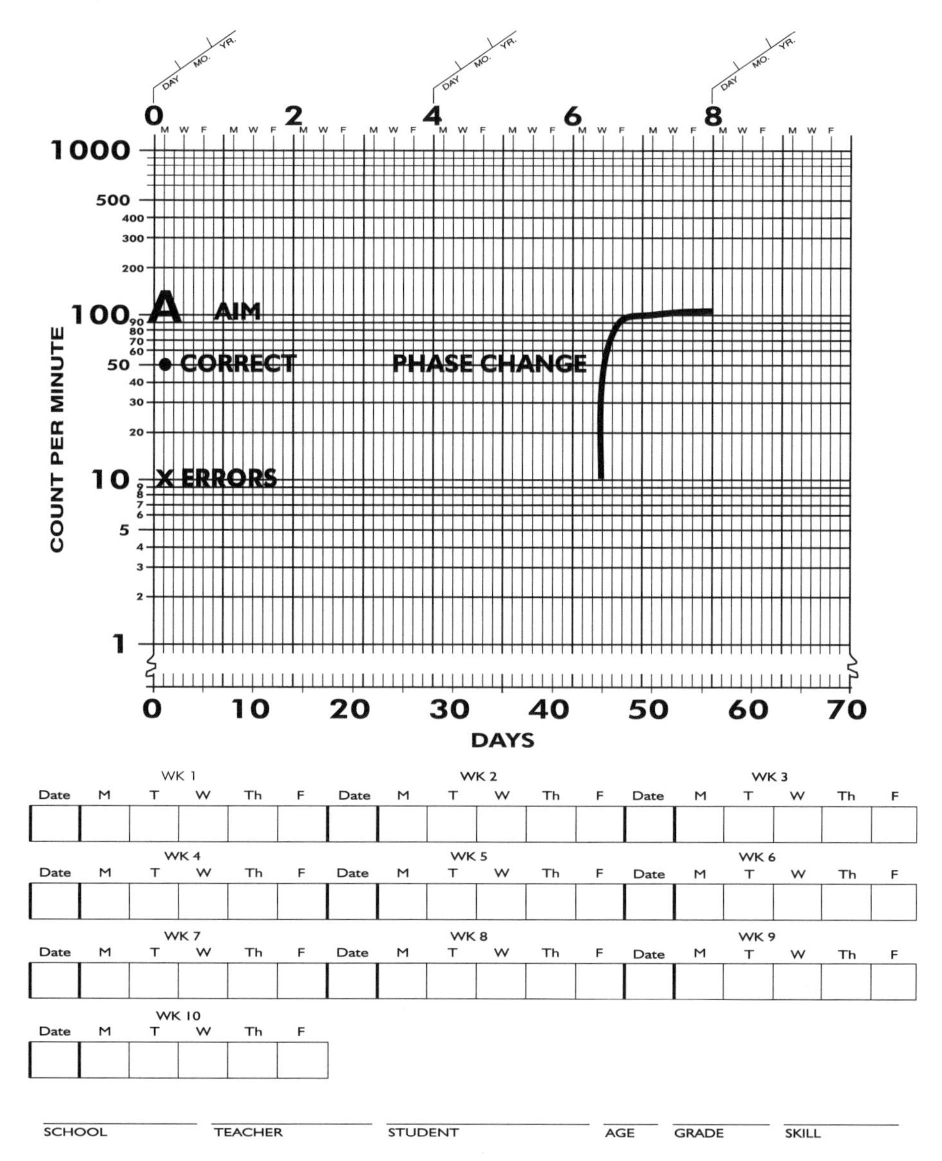

7. Individual dots (corrects) and Xs (errors) represent *daily performance* statements (number of corrects and errors per minute) and indicate how the student did on a particular task at a specific time (date). For example, a performance statement might be of the student who read 185 correct wpm with six errors on Thursday, November 16th.

8. As daily performance statements change across time (weeks) they become *weekly learning* statements and can be visually displayed using a trend line, which is a line drawn through a set of data that best represents the direction of responses. The improvement,

assuming the corrects are increasing, is expressed as weekly growth or improvement statements. If the correct responses doubled from the first to the second week, they would be expressed as x 2 (times 2), meaning that there was a 100% improvement from Week 1 to Week 2. In math, if a student increased his median correct responses in multiplication facts from 50 to 80, his growth statement for the two weeks would be x 1.60 (times 1.60) or a 60% improvement.

Another way of looking at improvement assumes a decrease in errors. In this case, a student decreased his errors from 30 to 20 per minute. Here the celeration would be considered a ÷ 1.50 (divide by 1.50) or a 50% reduction in errors.

9. Trend lines are drawn through a series of daily performance statements to visually display, as well as to mathematically calculate, progress ... or lack of progress. In the Precision Teaching model the trend line can be displayed by placing a #2 pencil or other straight object over the direction of the data or drawing a line freehand through the data. Either of these methods should give the teacher an idea of a student's progress, whether it is improving, worsening, or maintaining, and be able to judge whether there is adequate weekly growth. For example, corrects growing at x 1.50 or 50% per week.

   We would hope that any student under a condition of "practice" would show a growth statement of at least 25% per week and more like 50% (x 1.50) per week. A x 1.50 angle or slope is depicted in Figure 13. The mathematical formula for determining the slope statement is done by dividing the median score of Week 1 (30) into the median score of Week 2 (45), which when carried two places yields a x 1.50 slope. Having said that, however, the most significant analysis is not so much the specific mathematical calculation, but whether or not the student is progressing in accord with the teacher's expectations.

Figure 13. Calculating Slope Statements

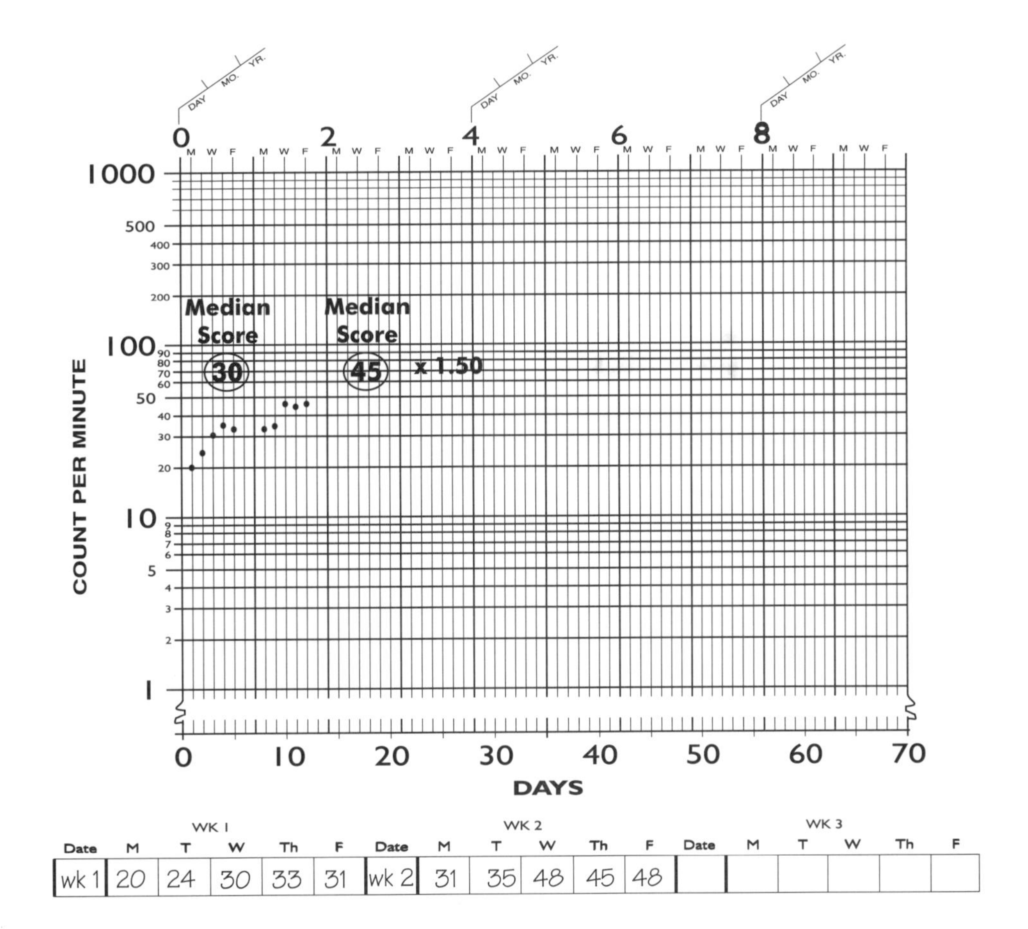

	WK 1						WK 2						WK 3				
Date	M	T	W	Th	F	Date	M	T	W	Th	F	Date	M	T	W	Th	F
wk 1	20	24	30	33	31	wk 2	31	35	48	45	48						

Interpreting the Dots

The next section is perhaps the most important part of the Precision Teaching model—the interpretation of the data and decisions that help the students become fluent. But before examining actual case studies, a quick review of the Precision Teaching Levels of Skill Development is necessary.

The idea behind the Levels of Skill Development matrix is to provide a visual display of the three stages: acquisition, practice, and fluency. Each stage or level has three elements: signs or signals to look for, suggestions for change, and the key decision (see Figure 14).

For example, if a student is struggling with "learning a basic concept," and has a low correct rate and high error rate, practice will have little, if any, effect. In this case, the student is in the acquisition stage and possibly needs more instruction. Another example is the student who has shown good growth and is beyond the acquisition stage but, for some reason, has leveled off far short of the fluency stage. The student is in the practice stage and possibly requires an incentive plan. The final example might include a student who has reached Aim, but then appears to have stopped growing. Here he has become fluent and probably needs a more challenging Skill Sheet.

Figure 14. Levels of Skill Development

ACQUISITION

- **Signs:**
  - Low rates of corrects with errors
  - A lot of daily bounce (variability)
  - No data patterns
- **Suggestions:**
  - Teach and model
  - Tool skill practice
  - Change Learning Channels
  - Take weight off
- **Key: TEACH**

PRACTICE

- **Signs:**
  - Middle rates of corrects
  - Daily growth in corrects
  - Less daily bounce
- **Suggestions:**
  - Instruct to errors
  - Consistent Learning Channels
  - Consistent format
  - Monitor and display
  - Incentives and rewards
- **Key: Provide PRACTICE**

FLUENCY

- **Signs:**
  - High rates of corrects (accuracy plus speed)
  - Automatic
  - Little daily bounce
  - Endurance
- **Suggestions:**
  - Change format
  - Change Learning Channels
  - Add weight
- **Key: MOVE ON**

Returning to interpretation of data and decision making, Figure 15 shows examples of student performances. The skill along with the Learning Channel (See/Write, See/Say, Think/Write, etc.) is identified at the top of the chart, the Aim is indicated by using the symbol A, corrects are depicted by dots, while errors are expressed using Xs.

An analysis of the data patterns needs to be made focusing on whether the student appeared to be improving, maintaining, or worsening, and whether there is a need to change, and if so, what kind of change to plan.

Once the one-minute timing has been scored, recorded, and charted, several questions should surface around interpretation and decision making. These might include:

1. Is there an overall Improving Pattern?
2. Has the student reached Aim two out of three trials?
3. Is there an overall Maintenance Pattern?
4. Is there little or no growth?
5. Is there a Worsening Pattern?

Questions like these should be asked when attempting to draw a causal relationship between environmental conditions and the academic performance of the student. Figure 15 shows examples of actual student data taken from Skill Sheets and one-minute timings.

The first example is a student who is practicing See/Write (S/W) add facts, sums to 18. The teacher determined the student was, at best, maintaining and needed to slice back to sums to 9. In the second illustration, the teacher decided that the student was improving, had reached Aim, demonstrated fluency, and was ready for more difficult material (e.g., x 9s). Each of the subsequent cases in Figure 15 show the data patterns and the decisions made.

Figure 15. Case Study Examples

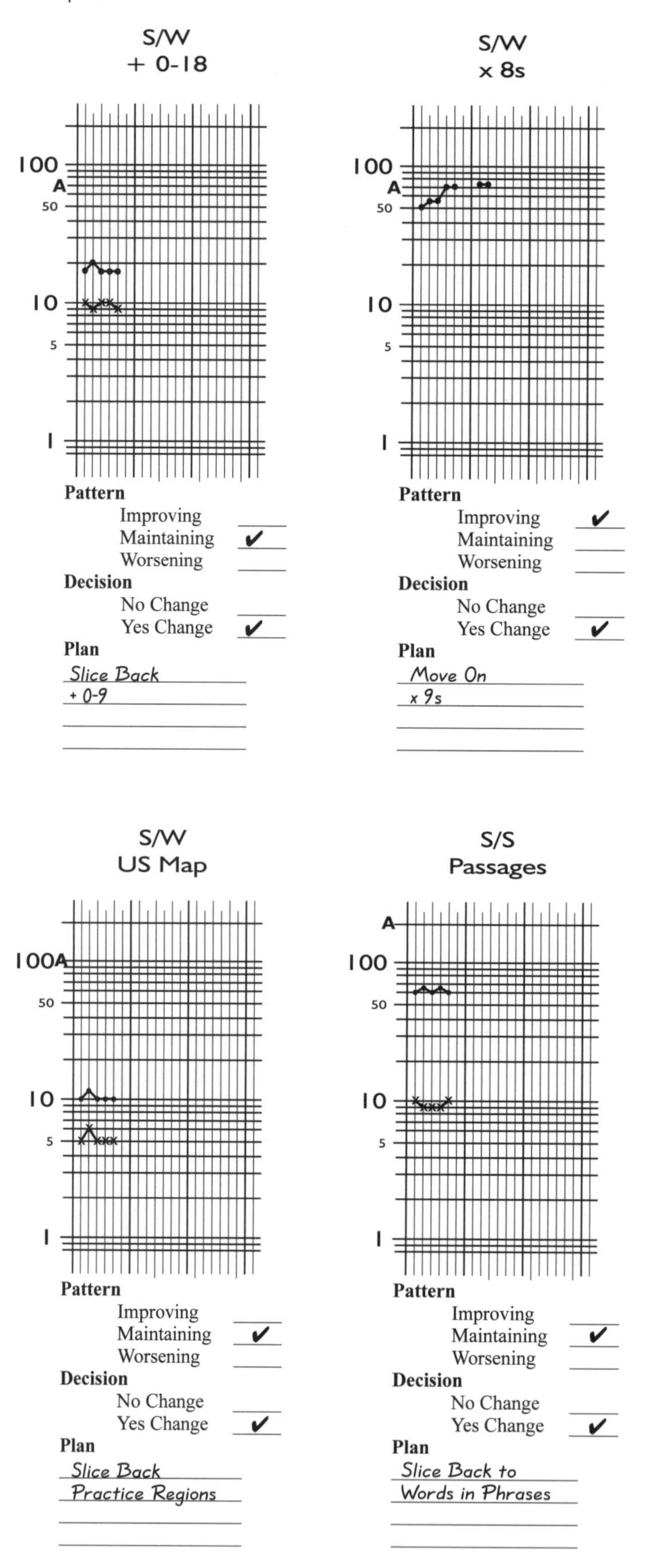

Figure 15. Case Study Examples (cont'd)

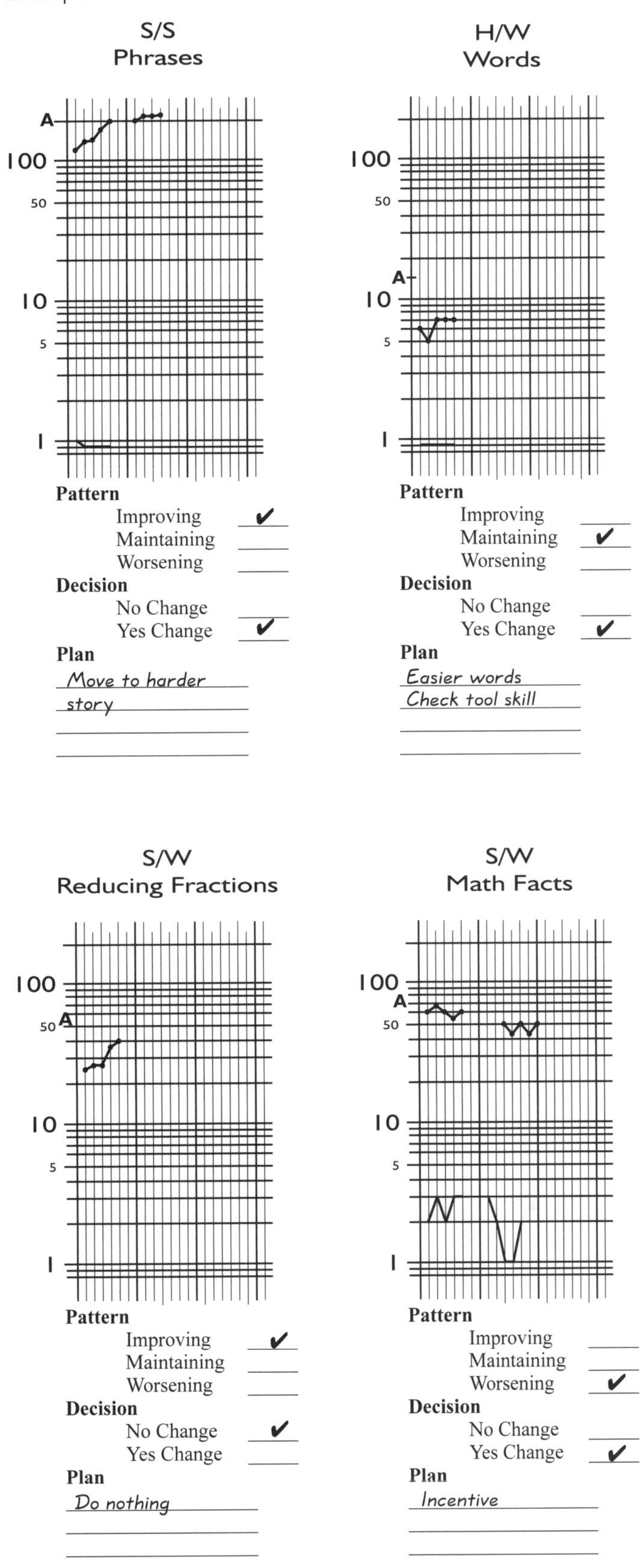

Figure 15. Case Study Examples (cont'd)

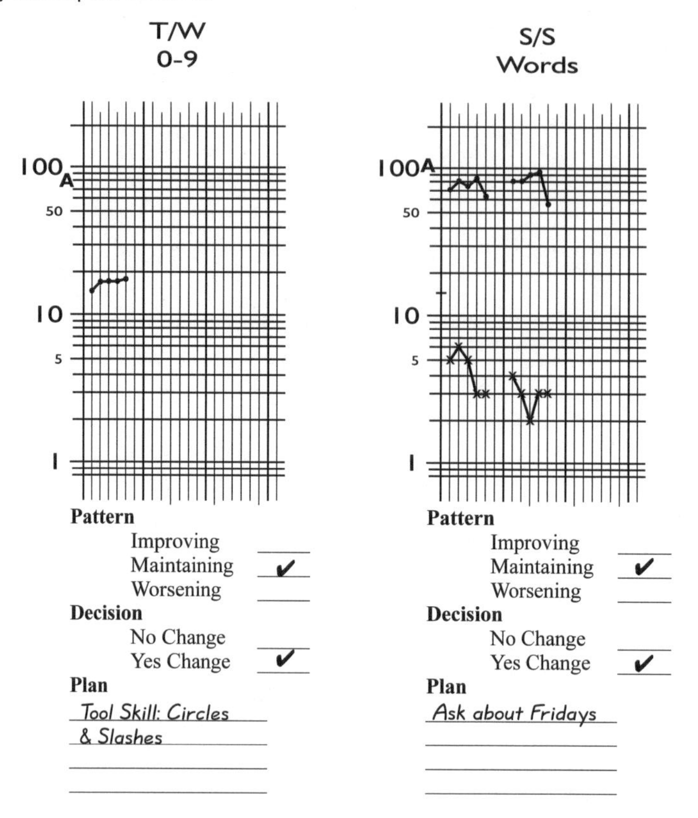

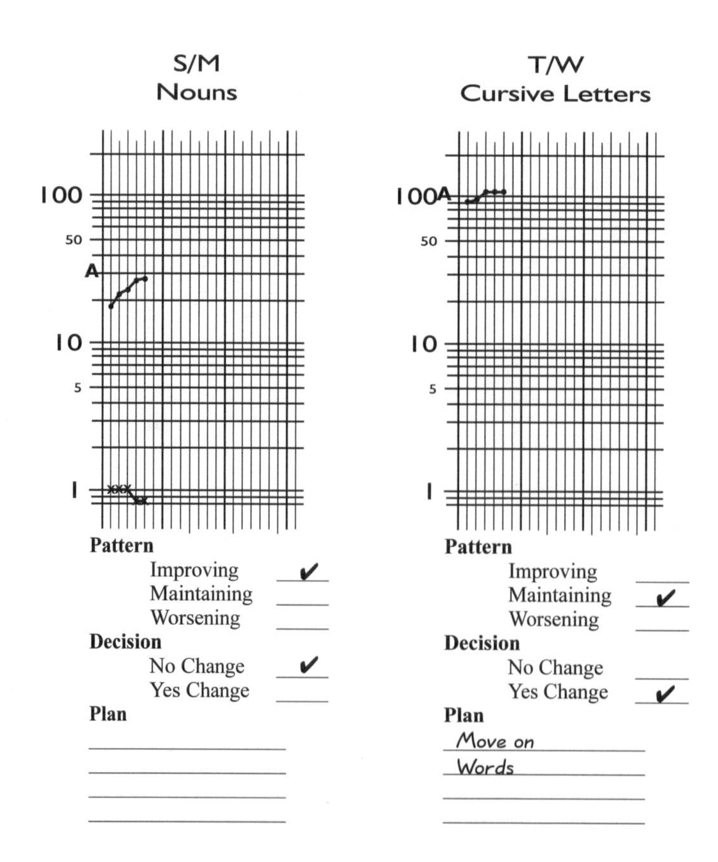

CHAPTER 3

Conducting the One-Minute Functional Assessment

Overview

In this chapter, you will learn how to conduct the One-Minute Functional Assessment. But first, here's a brief overview of how the functional assessment process proceeds.

1. **Monitor Student Performance to get a Baseline.** It is crucial that you know how well students are currently performing so that you can assess whether they improve with your assistance.

2. **Evaluate Student Performance.** Once we know how the student is performing, we need to determine if level and rate of progress is satisfactory or if changes are needed to increase the rate of learning.

3. **Analyze the Learner.** If the rate of progress is not satisfactory, then we will analyze the learner to determine the *reason* for the lack of progress.

4. **Teach with Precision.** If we make the decision to modify instruction *for a particular student*, then what type of instructional modification is *most effective*? Here it is important to have a list of validated best practices which have been shown to increase student performance. We must use those proven strategies with precision in order to assess their effectiveness.

General Considerations in Conducting a Functional Assessment

Teaching and functional assessment have some similarities in that good teachers try different strategies, evaluate student performance, and make needed changes. Many teachers already engage in these activities routinely and therefore will be familiar with the tool skills needed to conduct functional assessment. However, there are some differences between good teaching and functional assessment. The differences revolve around one theme: being systematic. With functional assessment, there is a need to be deliberate in the teaching and assessment process. Why? Because the goal is to identify factors that influence a student's learning. By being systematic, we can increase our certainty that the student is making some progress and that what we changed caused the improvement. Hence, when moving from the teaching mind-set to the functional assessment mind-set, the following principles apply.

1. **Administer Precision Teaching skill sheets the same way each time.** As much as possible, have the child complete the skill sheets under the same conditions each time. Small changes can make a big difference. The sheets should be given at the same time of day, using the same seating arrangement, and using the same instructions. If you decide to remind the child to get back to work whenever he stops working, then do this each time. Giving the skill sheets just before recess could produce much different results than giving the skill sheets following recess.

2. **Obtain a stable baseline.** To determine what works you need to be able to compare a student's performance using your usual or current teaching methods with the student's performance using a new method of teaching. Keeping track of the student's performance for a few sessions prior to trying something new is called the "baseline performance." The key to functional assessment is getting a good baseline. This is important because when a change is made, the effect of the change on a student's performance will be evaluated relative to that same student's past performance in baseline. With functional assessment, the goal is to look at progress compared to how the student *was* performing.

Those who are already using *Basic Skill Builders* sheets as part of their normal teaching will have been monitoring student performance and a special baseline period is not required. Those who wish to use *Basic Skill Builders* sheets for functional assessment will typically need to collect a minimum of three samples of student performance before proceeding with a change in instruction, although more may be required.

3. **Change one thing at a time.** If too many things are different each time the student performs on the skill sheets, and the student's performance changes, then we don't know which factor produced the change. In teaching, it is sometimes useful to be "creative," change the routine, or offer some variety to the students. While conducting a functional assessment, such changes can produce unpredictable results. One teacher, for example, decided to provide 10 minutes of additional practice time because a student was not making progress in two-digit addition facts. At the same time, the teacher changed the skill from two-digit addition to one-digit addition. The student's performance improved a lot! But was this improvement due to the extra practice, or was it due to using an easier skill? It is impossible to tell.

   Functional assessment will help to make teaching easier by quickly identifying what works, trying one technique at a time. Sometimes it makes sense to use a combination of techniques to produce a quick effect. Whenever you change two or three things at the same time, you will usually get a positive effect. But this often leads to wasted teacher and student energy because it is usually only one of the techniques which is actually producing the effect. In the above example, maybe using easier math problems was the only change needed. Or maybe the student could have started to improve in the more difficult math facts with some additional practice. The following guidelines for conducting functional assessment sessions are designed to improve both the efficiency and quality of your results.

How to Conduct the One-Minute Functional Assessment

Step 1: Monitor Student Performance to Obtain Baseline

The functional assessment process begins by carefully measuring student performance each day. This means that a skill sheet is given to the student each day and the result is recorded on the Standard Celeration or the 3 Cycle Academic Chart (sometimes referred to as "dropping the dots" because each entry on the chart resembles a dot). For those of you who are using Precision Teaching skill sheets, your job is mostly complete. You are already "dropping dots" so you have a consistent measure of student performance.

There are four ways students perform during this baseline period (see Figure 16).

Figure 16. Examples of the most common types of performance during baseline

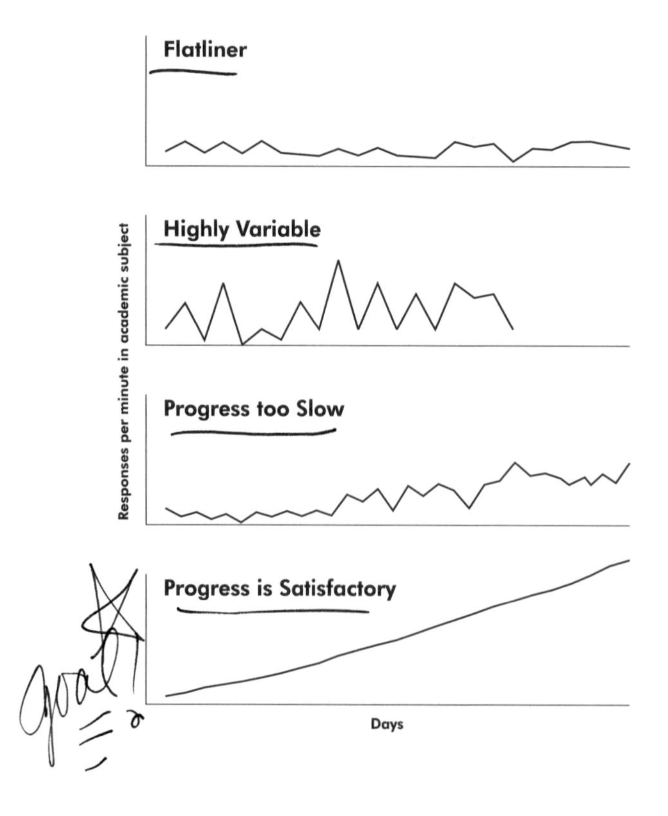

The "flatliner" chart is the most common. The student's performance is very stable from day to day, but his rate of progress is very "flat," meaning he is not improving. The "highly variable" chart is less common, but it will be seen occasionally in classrooms. This student's performance has a lot of variability, but overall, his average performance does not improve. Hence, this student would also be a concern. The "progress too slow" chart shows a student whose performance is stable and is even improving slightly, but the rate of improvement is below expectation and considered to be unsatisfactory.

Step 2: Evaluate Student Performance

Once we know how a student is performing, the next step is to determine if this level of performance is a problem. A problem exists when performance differs from expectations. It is *expected* that a child will progress 25% per week. An alternative to the formula described in Chapter 2 is to calculate the percentage by first subtracting the student's previous week's score from her score for this week. Then divide the result of that by the student's previous week's score. Finally, multiply that result by 100 to obtain a percentage. If that number is less than 25%, then the student has not made sufficient progress, and you should consider proceeding to Step 3. If the child has increased more than 25%, then the student's progress is considered to be good (see Figure 17).

Of course, common sense should be applied. If the child has been absent, or if school activities (e.g., assemblies, etc.) have interrupted teaching and student practice, then it would not be appropriate to expect a 25% progress rate. Similarly, a student may have had an isolated "down" day during the week because of illness or other factors. For these reasons, teachers will sometimes consider a child for functional assessment based upon two consecutive weeks where progress has been less than 25%.

Figure 17. Flow Chart of Functional Assessment Activity

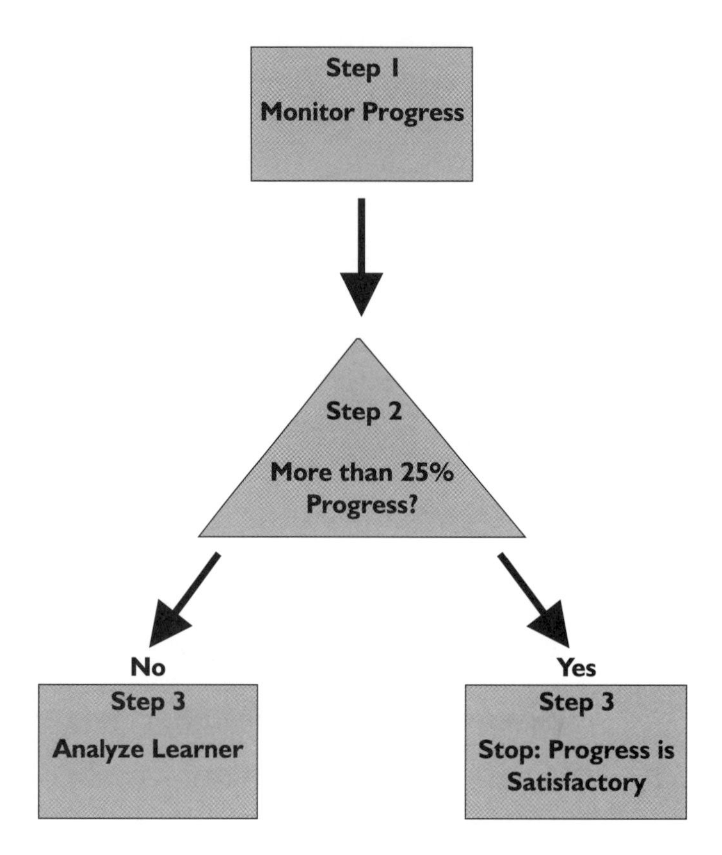

Step 3: Analyze the Learner

After collecting data on the child's performance and after determining that the child's performance is below expectations, the next step is to analyze the learner to better understand how to improve performance.

In analyzing the learner, we want to find things *under the teacher's control* which make a difference in a student's performance (see Table 3).

Table 3. Focus on Things Under Your Control

Under Teacher's Control	Not Under Teacher's Control
Amount of Practice	Intelligence
Level or Difficulty of Work	Brain Functioning
Seating Arrangement	Family Problems
Grading or Not Grading	Temperament
Learning Channel	Prior Education

One problem in considering factors that are not under the teacher's control is that they lead to solutions which are indirect and ineffective. What would you do with the knowledge that a student's IQ is 80 vs. 100? Can you improve the student's intelligence as a way to help him read with greater fluency? It can't be done. Similarly, even if you could change the student's family dynamic, it might not lead to improvements in her reading. On the other hand, changing the Learning Channel by allowing a student to say rather than write the answers to math facts is simple, under your control, and it may help improve the student's performance.

Our approach to finding out what works for a student is quite simple and direct, something that is so practical that it may seem odd at first. This approach to understanding the student is to *improve the student's performance*. When you can change a student's performance, you understand the student in the exact way that you need to understand the student as a teacher. You understand how to help him or her learn. For example, one could spend many hours finding creative ways to "understand" whether a student was really motivated. Yet, the quickest way to determine if a student is really doing his best on his math sheet is to compare his usual performance on the math sheets with his performance when we enhance his motivation. If he improves his performance, then we can say that he was not doing his best before and that incentives help. Of the many other ways to find out whether the student is motivated (e.g., we could talk to him or give him a motivation test), none are quicker or better than actually motivating the student and examining changes in performance. A simple intervention is your best form of assessment—better than *any* test. So our general approach will be to make an *educated* guess about what is wrong with the student and then try to *do something* about the problem. If we improve the student by motivating him or her or by teaching him or her differently, then whatever we are doing differently is the *key* to his or her problem. We can use this key to unlock his or her learning problem.

The idea then, after monitoring performance for at least three sessions, is to try a new procedure with a student, usually for no longer than a week. At the end of the week, examine the student's performance and assess if the new procedure has improved the student's performance. If not, try another technique, and keep doing so until the student's performance improves.

An example may help to illustrate this process. Mr. McGuffey has been keeping an eye on the daily performance of two students in his second grade class, Dick and Jane. These two students are both performing at a rate of about 40 digits per minute during the one-minute timed math Skill Sheet (Addition Facts: Sums to 10). Mr. McGuffey is concerned because for these students the skill level is too low (i.e., they should be working on more advanced skills), and yet their rate of progress is also unsatisfactory (see Figure 18). Mr. McGuffey places both students in a nondistracting area of the classroom to work and begins by enhancing instruction that occurs *prior* to the performance on the Skill Sheet by having Dick and Jane play a math game which increases practice (i.e., opportunities to respond correctly to math facts). This has a very positive effect on Dick but no effect on Jane. Next, Mr. McGuffey stops the math game and tells Dick and Jane that they can earn 10 minutes of time on the computer *after* the completion of the timed skill sheet if they are able to obtain two more correct than they did the day before. Jane's performance jumps immediately, but using computer time as an incentive had no effect on Dick.

Figure 18. Results of Mr. McGuffey's Work With Dick and Jane in Math

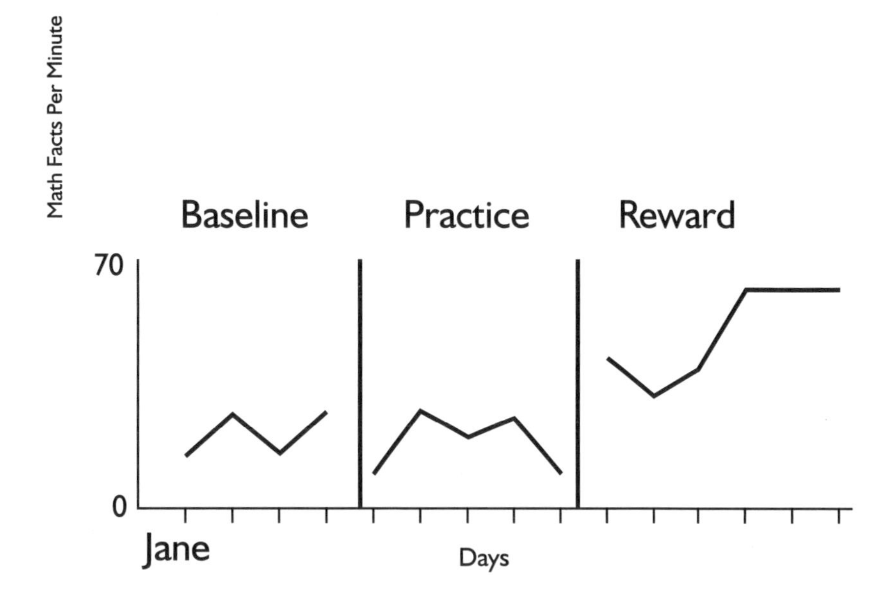

From this analysis, it can be concluded that the two students who were performing at the same level needed different kinds of help. Jane can clearly do the work if it matters to her. The consequence of extra computer time caused improved math performance to matter to Jane. Dick simply can't improve without additional instruction in the form of practice. Jane's needs, then, are in the form of consequences. Dick's needs are for increased opportunities to practice.

Where do these good ideas for improving performance come from? Many teachers, given their training and experience, have a storehouse of techniques that they use for improving student performance. Functional assessment provides a means to *evaluate* those techniques for their effectiveness. After monitoring a student during a baseline period, then carefully implementing a technique for a week, are you seeing a 25% increase in performance? If not, try something else from your storehouse of techniques.

An example may help to illustrate this process. Ms. Jackson had two students, Jeff and Marcel, whose spelling performances needed improvement. Ms. Jackson, based upon success with this technique in the past, decided to send notes home with the students about improving their spelling performances. After first collecting data for three days on Jeff and Marcel, Ms. Jackson sent notes home with them like the one in Figure 19.

Figure 19. Ms. Jackson's Note to a Student's Parents

Dear Mr. and Mrs. Samules:

In class we are doing spelling words each week. The spelling list for this week is attached. During the last three weeks, Marcel has received a score of 70, 72, and 55 out of 100. I think he can do better than this. If you have time to help him with his spelling this week, that would be a great help. You can have him write each word in the list twice and then give him an oral spelling test. As Marcel spells each word, correct him if he makes a mistake.

Some parents offer a small treat (favorite snack) or extra privilege (staying up late on Friday night) if their child is able to improve his or her best score by 3 points. I think this might be a good incentive for Marcel, too.

Thank you for your help.

Ms. Jackson

The charts for Jeff and Marcel are shown in Figure 20. Sending a note home worked well for both children.

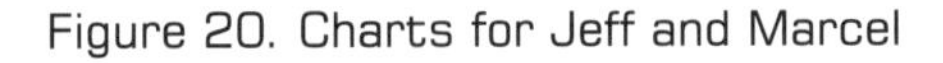
Figure 20. Charts for Jeff and Marcel

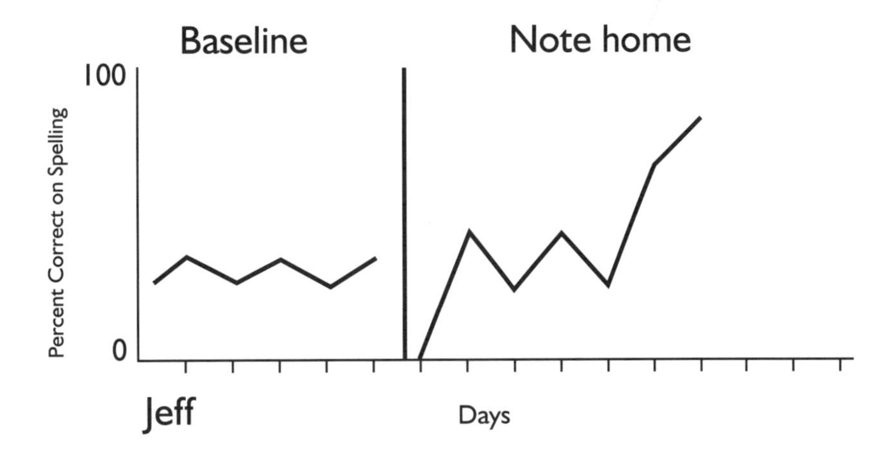

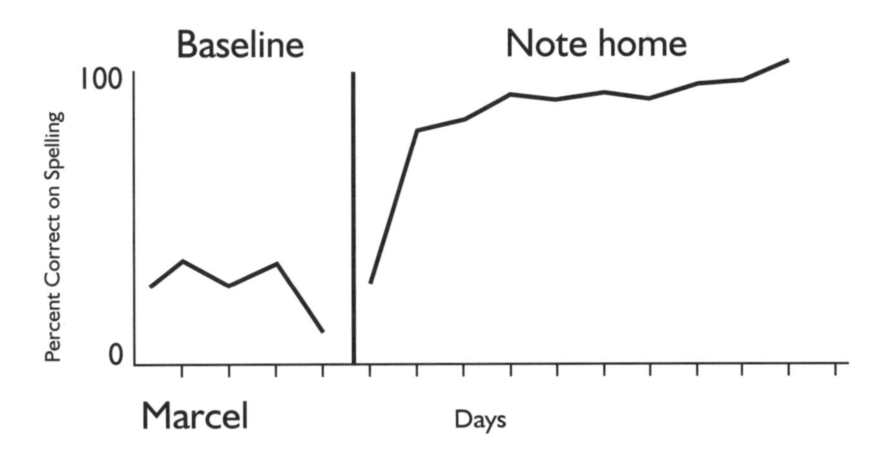

The Functional Assessment Grid, originally presented in Chapter 1 (see Figure 1), is another source of good ideas. The idea is to maximize factors that improve student performance, such as instruction and feedback, while minimizing factors that detract from performance, such as noise, a pesky peer, or even teacher attention for the wrong thing.

Some teachers will not know where to begin with a particular student or will run through their best techniques and still not bring about any change in a student's performance. Other teachers may prefer to begin with a more structured process for finding what works for a student. The systematic process can begin by first examining the four basic reasons children fail to progress.

1. The student can't do or won't do the work,

2. The material is too hard,

3. The student needs more practice, and

4. The student needs more help.

The reasons have been placed in an order, which based upon our experience, are the easiest and most likely to yield beneficial results to the student.

Reason #1: Can't Do versus Won't Do. There are two, and only two, reasons a student does not perform academic work: he either can't do it or he won't do it. That means he either lacks the skills to do the work or he simply prefers not to do the work. It is advisable to begin the functional assessment process by performing a quick check to determine if the student has a Won't Do problem as outlined in Figure 21.

Figure 21. Can't Do versus Won't Do Assessment

Step 1: After getting three to five days of the student's usual baseline performance on the same Skill sheet, take the child aside and say, "During the last three days on your math sheet, your highest score has been _____. Today, if you beat that score, I am going to let you __________ (earn a prize, free time, or something the student indicates she truly would like). Do you understand?"

Step 2: Administer the skill sheet.

Step
3: Determine number correct.

Step
4: Decide. If the student's performance with incentives is 15-20% greater than his or her best performance, then consider the student to have a won't do problem.

If you are successful at this step, stop. There is no need to continue looking for additional problems. The student *can* do the work and that is all you need to know.

Reason # 2: The material is too hard. If you fail to detect a Won't Do problem with the "Can't Do versus Won't Do" assessment, then the student probably has a Can't Do problem or skill deficit. The first step is to determine the *type* of skill deficit by using the methods suggested in Precision Teaching. You can:

— **Slice back**: Move back in the skill sequence to an easier skill.

— **Check tool skill**: Make sure the student can adequately perform all of the tool skills required and possibly switch to a tool skill for daily practice instead of the skill now being attempted.

— **Change Learning Channel**: Occasionally a change in the Learning Channel will make the skill easier for the student to perform. In some cases, a change in Learning Channel is related to tool skills. A positive increase in performance by changing from See/Write to See/Say math facts might mean that the tool skill of writing needs work. For more information on reducing skill difficulty see Chapter 2 or the *Basic Skill Builders* book (Sopris West).

Figure 22. The Material is Too Hard Assessment

Step 1: Use the skill sheet on which the student is currently assigned.

Step 2: Collect at least three days of baseline data. Baseline means that you use the skill sheets for a daily one-minute timing and use no special instructional procedures with the student.

Step 3: Begin the intervention phase where you slice back to lower skill levels. Stop slicing back when you reach a skill level where the child is accurate and reasonably fluent.

Step 4: Monitor progress for at least one week.

Step 5: Evaluate progress. Did the student increase by at least 25% over the course of the week? If so, then you have discovered that skill level at which the student is ready to practice.

Step 6: If this test had positive results, consider slicing back the skill. If this is not practical (e.g., as would be the case if all students in the class are working on the same skill), also conduct a check for Reason #4, "The Student Needs More Help" in order to determine if the student's skill level can be increased with a little additional assistance.

To conduct this test, *baseline* consists of the student's performance using the currently assigned (i.e., too difficult) skill and the *intervention phase* consists of the new easier skill. If the work being assigned was too difficult, then you should see an immediate jump in the student's performance. Figure 23 shows a graph for Joan who showed a positive result when she was sliced back from x5 in multiplication to x2.

Figure 23. Effect on Joan for Slicing Back

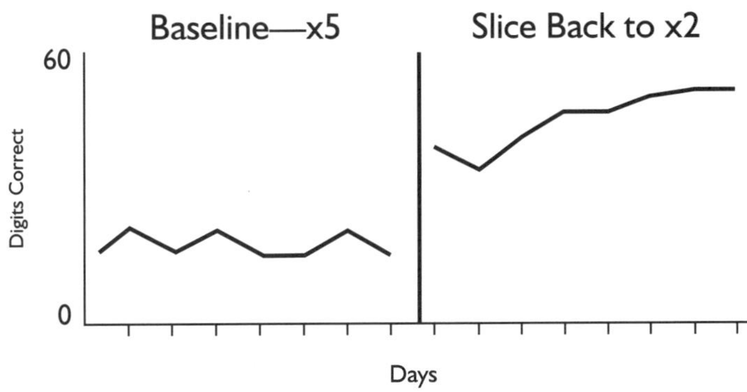

If a positive result is not obtained with the first slice back, then it may be necessary to continue to slice back until results are obtained. This process is illustrated in Figure 24 with Juan.

Figure 24. Results of Slicing Back for Juan

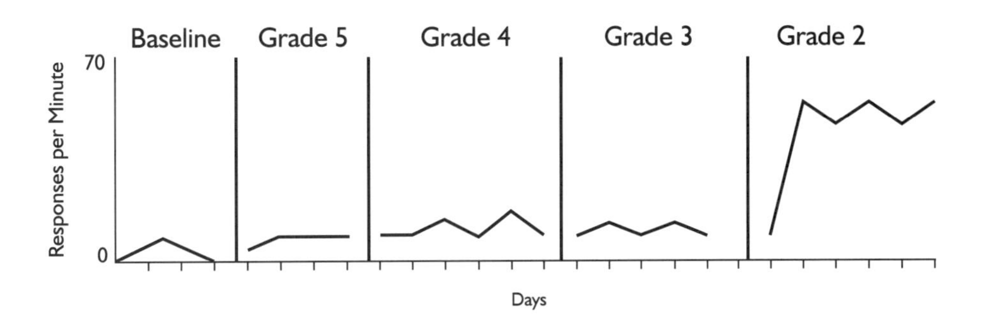

Once again, it is important that you check for Reason #1, the Won't Do problem, *before* you check for this problem. Some students with the Won't Do problem are preferring not to do the work because it is *slightly* too difficult. If the material were a little easier, then they would do the work. In other words, they have the motivation to do easy work but not difficult work. By reducing the difficulty level, a Won't Do problem can look like a Can't Do problem. Therefore, always check for Won't Do problems first.

Reason #3: The Student Needs More Practice. Logically, a major reason a student does not progress is because he does not practice enough. The experienced piano teacher can easily tell whether her pupil has practiced as prescribed or not. Similarly, most classroom teachers know if practice is occurring. Practice is a very important part of the teaching/learning process. Ideally, teachers will spend approximately 10-20% of the time allocated for a subject in teaching the student by telling, modeling, and demonstrating. This is called *establishing the skill.* Once the student is capable of performing the skill accurately, then instructional time should shift to practice time. Teachers should then be spending approximately 80% of the time allocated for practicing the subject. This is called *building fluency* with the skill. A teacher in the "detective" mode will suspect that the student needs more practice when they see a student who is relatively accurate in the performance of a skill but performs the skill at a slow rate. For example, insufficient opportunities to practice might be suspected of a student who has been reading a third-grade passage with 100% accuracy for the last week but has been reading only 20 wpm with no increase in rate of words read.

Using the functional assessment process to test for the possibility that practice will help a student proceeds in a very straightforward manner. The process is described in Figure 25.

Figure 25. The Student Needs More Practice

Step

1: Use skill sheet on which the student is accurate but not fluent. This will usually mean that the student will be accurate 90% of the time or greater and the student's fluency level will generally be in the lower end of the fluency range.

Step

2: Collect at least three days of baseline data. Baseline means that you use your own teacher-developed sheet or the *Basic Skill Builders* sheets for a daily one-minute timing and use no special instructional procedures with the child.

Step 3: Begin the intervention phase where you provide increased opportunities to practice the skill using a series of one-minute timings. The easiest intervention will be to allow the student to practice the skill sheets three to five additional times each day. A number of other strategies are presented in Chapter 6.

Step 4: Monitor progress for at least one week.

Step 5: Evaluate progress. Did the student's progress increase by at least 25% over the course of the week? If so, then providing more opportunities to practice is a benefit to the student.

Step 6: If this test had positive results, consider using one or more of the strategies in Chapter 5 to increase practice opportunities for the student.

Reason #4: The Student Needs More Help. We have placed this one at the bottom of our list of possible reasons because it can be the most difficult to check out. Practice does not help if the student is not practicing the skill accurately. In fact, practice can hurt students in terms of decreased motivation or learning to perform the skill in a manner which is wrong. Students who are not accurate need help learning the skill. Figure 26 describes the process for determining if a student needs more help and the teaching strategies to help the student.

Figure 26. The Student Needs More Help

Step 1: Use a skill sheet on which the student is having difficulty. That is, the student is neither accurate nor fluent. You would select such a skill only if there is some reason to improve accuracy on *this* particular difficult skill rather than slice back to an easier skill.

Step 2: Collect at least three days of baseline data. Baseline means that you use the same skill sheets for a daily one-minute timing and use no special instructional procedures with the child.

Step 3: Begin the intervention phase where some additional assistance is provided to the student. Ideas for how to provide help to the student can be found in Chapter 6. As an ideal assessment, you would typically combine two or more of the procedures for a short period of time. For example, the Nuclear Reading Intervention (see Table 5) is a combination of strategies for providing more assistance to a student in reading. It includes modeling (listening passage preview) and feedback (error correction) as well as opportunities to practice the skill.

Step 4: Monitor progress for at least one week.

Step 5: Evaluate progress. Did the student's progress increase by at least 25% over the course of the week? If so, then providing additional assistance is a benefit to the student.

Step 6: If this test had positive results, consider using one or more of the strategies in Chapter 6 to increase practice opportunities for the student. Or, if you have incorporated many types of help, as opposed to just one type, in your assessment, then you might consider cutting out one or more of the components to determine if you can have similar benefits with less help.

 4: Teach With Precision

Once you have analyzed the learner, the most difficult part of functional assessment is complete. If you have examined one or more possible reasons for a lack of student progress and have obtained a positive result (i.e., the student's performance improved), then you are ready to use the results of the functional assessment to guide future teaching or intervention efforts. Table 4 shows you how to interpret and link the assessment results to intervention. For example, if you found that the reason the student was not performing was a Won't Do problem, then you will be directed to an explanation of this result, some general intervention needs, as well as some specific intervention ideas.

Table 4. Linking Assessment Results to Intervention Ideas

Assessment Results	Test	Result	Explanation	Intervention Needs	Intervention Ideas
Student won't do	Test for Reason #1: Does motivation help?	Performance improved when reinforced	Student can do work but only if motivated	• Reduce Effort • Increase Motivation • Increase Interest	• Mystery Motivator • Beat your last score • Goal setting • Thirty-Second Trials • (See Chapter 4 for more ideas.)
Material is too Hard	Test for Reason #2: Does the use of easier materials help?	Performance improves with easy material	Student can't do assigned work because it is too difficult	• Slice Back • Change Tool Skill • Change Learning Channel	• Assess tool skills and teach them first if needed • Break task into smaller steps • "Sandwich" easy work with more difficult work

Table 4. Linking Assessment Results to Intervention Ideas (continued)

Assessment Results	Test	Result	Explanation	Intervention Needs	Intervention Ideas
Student needs practice	Test for Reason #3: Does additional practice help?	Practice improved performance	Student is accurate but not fluent	• Daily Practice to Improve Fluency	• Increase student's work pace • Alter Learning Channel • Spread probes all during the day • Peer tutoring (See Chapter 5 for more ideas.)
Student needs more help	Test for Reason #4: Does providing additional assistance help?	Performance improved when assistance was provided	Prompting, modeling, telling, etc. are needed for student to perform at higher level	• Prompting • Cuing • Modeling • Feedback	• Tell student the steps • Model the steps • Provide feedback as student does steps (See Chapter 6 for more ideas.)

In Chapters 4, 5, and 6, you will find strategies and techniques that have proven to be successful in addressing the various reasons students fail to progress. Each of these chapters corresponds to one of the reasons for a lack of progress discussed in this chapter, with the exception of the reason "The Material is too Hard." The simple intervention strategy for this reason, slicing, is all that is necessary.

Maintaining Student Performance

The analysis of student performance told us what works for a particular student. The final step is to adapt instruction so that what works for a student becomes something that student routinely receives. But if what works for one student is applicable to more students or fits within existing classroom routines, it is more likely to be used on a regular basis. Teachers will typically only use functional assessment to evaluate modifications that they know they can readily adopt into classroom routine. In an earlier example, Mr. McGuffey was pleased that he had found something effective for Jane. However, he was not happy about the prospect of providing 10 minutes of extra computer time every day for just one student. Given that he was comfortable with only using extra computer time for Jane two to three days per week, he used a Mystery Motivator (Rhode, Jenson, & Reavis, 1993) so that Jane could continue earning computer time but on a random basis and not every time she met her goal.

Maintaining and managing instruction, especially if it is somewhat individualized for various children can present challenges to the teacher. It has been suggested that each classroom contains a number of resources (e.g., peers, etc.) that can be put to good use when starting instructional programs which are more than the teacher can handle alone. Various interventions of the type we are recommending can be made more manageable by getting yourself some help and making use of the available resources. The individual cells of Table 5 are examples of the types of strategies which are available to teachers. The creative teacher can then adapt this table's suggestions to find hundreds of ways to make instruction more varied and interesting while making the job of teaching easier.

Table 5. Nuclear Reading Intervention

	Type of Intervention		
CHANGE AGENTS	**CONSEQUENCES** Changing What Comes After Instruction	**ANTECEDENTS** Changing What Comes Before or During Instruction	**TEACHING** Changing the Method of Instruction
Self (Student)	Self-charting of number correct each day Self-reinforcement (students put their own stickers on chart)	Students can move themselves to a quiet area if they feel distracted	Students drill themselves with flash cards
Peer	Playing with a peer after meeting academic goal Students score each other's assignments	Students work in small groups and the groups set daily goals	Students take turns explaining meaning of a story to each other
Home	Parents provide reinforcement at home for good work at school	Parents are asked to ensure children get enough sleep and a good breakfast	Parents review homework and drill children on problems missed

Table 5. Nuclear Reading Intervention (continued)

	Type of Intervention		
CHANGE AGENTS	**CONSEQUENCES** Changing What Comes After Instruction	**ANTECEDENTS** Changing What Comes Before or During Instruction	**TEACHING** Changing the Method of Instruction
Teacher	Teachers provide free time at end of day for students who met their goals	Teachers decrease transition time in reading to allow for more opportunities to practice	Teachers maintain fast paced lessons to maintain interest and provide for more student responding
Computer	Computer time is used to reinforce students who met their math goals	Computer provides a two-minute "warm up" activity to "get kids thinking" before doing their daily skill sheets	Computer provides additional practice with feedback on vocabulary words

Maintaining student performance involves taking the techniques which functional assessment has identified to be effective and using them in the classroom on a regular basis. The monitoring of student progress is extended using Precision Teaching one-minute timings throughout the school year and changes in the student's program are made if needed. It is important to emphasize that we must expect that students will change. Strategies which were once effective may no longer be effective as the student's skill level improves. By monitoring student performance, it can be determined quickly when student performance gains are in need of attention. When using skill sheets with the entire class, teachers "take the pulse" of the class on a regular basis. They know who is really behind and who is ahead. They can ensure that all students are working at their level and this alone greatly boosts student performance.

Sources:

Daly, E., Witt, J., Mortens, B., & Dool, E. (1997). A model for conducting a functional analysis of academic performance problems. *School Psychology Review, 26,* 554-574.

Rhode, G., Jenson, W., & Reavis, K. (1993). *The tough kid book*. Longmont, CO: Sopris West.

CHAPTER 4

Intervention and Teaching Strategies When:
The Student Won't Do the Work

There are many ways to help a student who tests positive for a Won't Do problem. A positive test result tells you that, under optimal conditions, the student *can* do the work. Many of the general and specific techniques suggested in this chapter do not involve providing the student with rewards. Rather, they involve increasing the importance of the task to the student. There are many ways to enhance student motivation. The use of positive consequences may come to mind first, but normally, the use of rewards is not the best starting point. Although rewards are often the most effective, they are sometimes the most bother to teachers. The goal is to find something practical that can be used in the classroom.

The following strategies provide a starting point. But, be creative, the teacher is the expert in the classroom and knows many things that can enhance student performance. It is important to continue taking data to ensure the strategies are working and are continuing to be effective. Choosing and using one of the strategies in this chapter is not the end of functional assessment. Instead, you continue your monitoring efforts and make changes as needed.

It is also important to keep in mind that Won't Do students are making a choice. They are choosing not to do work they are capable of doing. Rewards for academic performance are one way to get them to make *their* choice the same as *your* choice. Another option, is to pay attention to what the student is doing instead and to make that option less attractive or unavailable. If the student is opting to talk to a peer rather than work, then move the peer. If the student is choosing to look out the window rather than working, then face his seat away from the window. These simple strategies are often as good as using consequences to produce desired results.

A Word About Inappropriate Behavior

Sometimes the concern of the teacher is a student's inappropriate behavior rather than learning. The functional assessment process will begin in the same way for behavior problems as for academic problems. We will first begin with finding strategies to help the student be successful academically. The research on behavior is very clear on two issues. First, a student is less likely to behave appropriately if he cannot do his main job of completing his academic work with a high success rate. If the material is too difficult, for example, and the student cannot perform the work with a reasonable degree of fluency, then the student will be more likely to engage in inappropriate behavior. Second, procedures which decrease inappropriate behaviors do not necessarily increase academic responding but increasing academic responding does decrease inappropriate behavior. Hence, for inappropriate behavior, the goal is to start with maximizing academic success and then responding to any behavioral concerns which remain.

General Strategies for the Student Who Won't Do the Work

Minimize Detractions, Distractions, and Disruptions

Students who are not performing up to their ability are usually not sitting and doing nothing. Instead they are looking around, talking to peers, annoying other students, etc. Make it easy for the student to focus on schoolwork by arranging the classroom environment to maximize success. Refer to Figure 27 to help you to think about what to minimize and maximize.

Figure 27. Functional Assessment Grid

	Maximize Activities	Minimize Activities
Before Performance	Effective Instructional Activities or Other Events	Detractions, Distractions, and Disruptions
After Performance	Effective Feedback or Consequences	Consequences which decrease academic performance

It is especially important to give close attention to the *decelerating* activities because these are things that happen in the classroom which keep performance low. It is usually easy to find out what is distracting the student.

Simply provide some work for the student to complete and see what she does instead.

If a student talks to her classmates, then, from a functional assessment perspective, we might say that peer attention is a consequence which is rewarding. Peer attention rewards a behavior, that is, talking, which is incompatible with designated schoolwork. The solution for a student who is talking instead of working might be to seat the student away from peers who may encourage off-task behaviors. If the student looks out the window, face his seat away from the window.

These same activities can be used to motivate the student. If he likes to talk to others, give him some free time with a friend *contingent* on meeting his goal on the daily skill sheets. If he likes to daydream, give him some time to do so when he does well.

The functional assessment process can be used to assess which of these strategies is most effective. The procedure is to provide the student with skill sheets under normal circumstances. Hence, the student would be given the sheets in his normal seat in the classroom at a time when seat work is typically assigned. Other students would be working on their normally assigned work. To make sure you have stable performance, repeat the test under normal conditions at least three times. Following that, try to enhance the student's ability to focus on the task and see if that helps. Figure 28 illustrates a teacher who first moved the student away from a disruptive peer and then moved the student a second time near the teacher's desk. The first strategy was not effective, but the second one did prove to be successful.

Figure 28. Moving a child away from peers as a way to improve performance

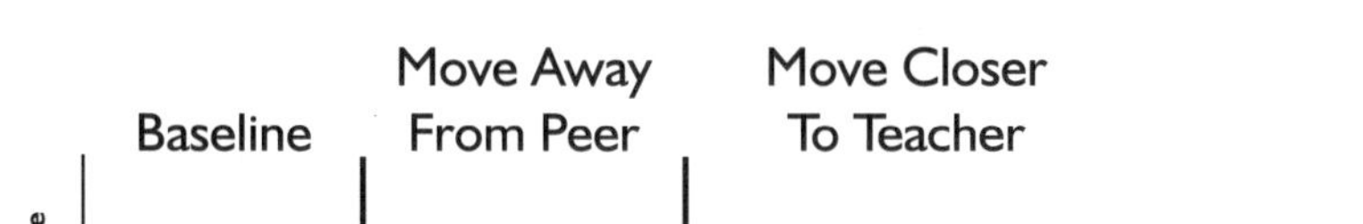

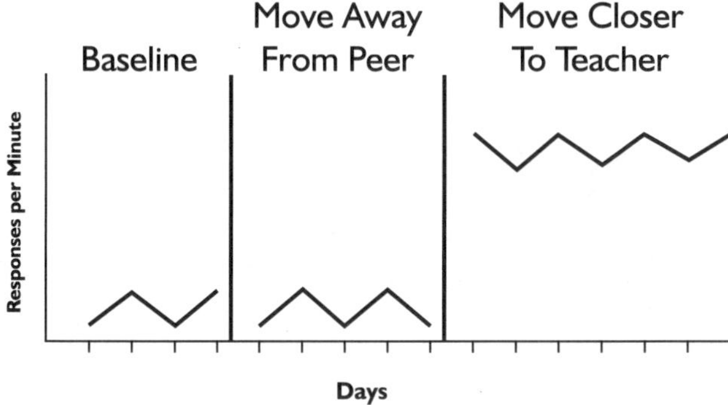

Use High-Interest Materials

Instructional materials often have a lot to do with how interested the student is in learning. For normal classroom assignments, it may be more effective if the materials are tied into what the student finds interesting. For reading, this may involve the use of high interest/low vocabulary materials. In math, this may require connecting the lessons to the student's life circumstance. Computations involving money may be more interesting than simple addition facts.

Choice

Research has shown that merely giving a student the choice of *what* to do or *when* to do it can produce dramatic results. This can be as simple as telling the student, "The spelling assignment and the math assignment must be completed within one hour. Which one would you like to do first?" Or it can be as simple as providing the student with a choice of stories to read and allowing him to choose. As an added bonus for teachers, allowing some student choice seems to have big benefits for behavioral improvement as well.

Use Shorter Sessions

The typical Precision Teaching skill sheets are based upon one minute sessions. Some students find it difficult to perform for even one minute. Using shorter sessions of 30 seconds and building up to the full minute in 10-second increments can improve performance for students who have difficulty staying on task.

Goal Setting

For some students, simply setting a goal (aim), without any offer of reward, is sufficient to obtain improvements in performance. However, some students will show even greater improvements if they are involved in determining the goal.

To use this technique, establish the goal (aim), perhaps with input from the student, then tell the student that you expect that she will get that number correct. Provide praise for accomplishing the goal and simply tell the student,

"Perhaps you will do better tomorrow" if the goal is not accomplished. The true agenda is to help the student shift from pleasing the teacher to self-satisfaction for doing good work.

Generally, the goal will be set such that modest improvements (e.g., 15-25% per week) are made. Alternatively, the goal may remain the same as the difficulty of the task increases.

The Stern Talk

Related to goal setting is a technique which is as old as teaching: the stern talk. When a student improves his performance to gain a reward, you can assume that he has not been trying his best prior to reward. When they see this, some teachers say to themselves, "Gotcha," meaning they caught the student not doing as well as she can. An easy first step then is to take the student aside at some point and say, "I have noticed that you have not been working as hard as you can. I know you can do much better and I expect you to buckle down and do your best." This is, of course, said with full eye contact and a stern voice.

Self-Monitoring

Students as young as first grade can be taught to record and manage their own progress and behavior. Show a student how to chart her daily performance on the skill sheets. This can be combined with goal setting by telling her, "The goal is to see the dots going up the page and not down." The student's chart should be placed in a visible location, such as on the cover of a folder. This may seem simple but monitoring your own progress means you have to notice and pay attention to your progress.

Mystery Motivator

A version of the Mystery Motivator can be used with skill sheets. To use this strategy you will need a clear colored felt-tip marking pen. The clear-colored pens usually come packaged in a variety pack with other colors. Using a clean *paper* copy of any skill sheet, make a distinctive mark on the sheet at a point which represents your target goal for the student. The mark could be a smiley face, the student's name, or whatever you prefer. The mark at this point will not be visible.

Present the paper to the student and explain that, if he works hard, he may earn the Mystery Motivator. Show him an envelope or box where the Mystery Motivator is secreted inside. Tell the student he can find out what the Mystery Motivator is only by doing well. Allow the student to work as usual for a one-minute timing.

Following that, allow the student to take a colored felt-tip marking pen, using any color other than clear, and shade in all the answer slots for the completed correct problems. If he finds the secret mark, then he is allowed to open the special Mystery Motivator envelope or box. Inside the envelope or box is a piece of paper on which you have written the reward he is to receive. The Mystery Motivator is a great intervention for many reasons. First, it works! Second, the teacher has total control over not only what the reward will be, but whether there will be a reward for that day at all. Third, small rewards can be very reinforcing to most students because of the "mystery" involved. Often, for students, discovery of what the mystery is can be as motivating as the reward itself. Finally, the frequency and size of the rewards can gradually be reduced by the teacher so that students are less dependent on the reward. An example of the Mystery Motivator follows in the section of this chapter on specific interventions for students who have a Won't Do problem.

Study Buddy

The idea behind this strategy is that sometimes kids can motivate kids. The process begins with peer tutoring. Of course, the tutor must have more skills than the tutee. Arrange something simple such as flash cards for the tutor to present to the tutee. Following instruction, a skill sheet is presented to the tutee. If the tutee does not meet the goal, then the teacher says the following to the tutor with the tutee present: "Are you going to let ______ get by with this kind of work? I know if you two work together you can meet the goal tomorrow."

If the goal is accomplished, both the tutor and the tutee get a reward. Neither one is rewarded if the goal is not accomplished.

School-Home Note

Parents can sometimes be a very effective resource. This strategy has several benefits. First, it provides a means to communicate with parents about something very concrete: how their child performed that day. Second, parents can provide rewards that are far beyond what teachers can provide. Third, the parents can be encouraged to help the child with skill problems.

The first step is a meeting with the parents where the idea is presented to them. They must agree to review the child's paper each day and, in most cases, provide a reward if performance is above a certain level. They can also be asked to help the child practice the skill, for example, by using flash cards.

The next step is to tell the child the procedure and to begin using it. Each day the child will be given a paper copy of a skill sheet. The teacher will conduct a one-minute timing as usual. The sheet will be scored and sent home with the child. From there, the parents carry out their end of the agreement.

Treasure Chest

For the very difficult to motivate, the treasure chest is an option. The treasure chest is just a box filled to the brim with "treasures" (e.g., pencils, small toys, and candies) that children in the specific grade would enjoy.

Use of the treasure chest is simple: the student is told that if he meets the goal, then he can choose one thing from the treasure chest. This intervention is virtually guaranteed to be effective for students who test positive for reward. If it does not work, the material may be too difficult and you would need to slice back the skill level.

SPECIFIC VALIDATED PRACTICES FOR STUDENTS WHO CAN DO THE WORK BUT WON'T DO THE WORK

Mystery Motivator to Increase Reading Performance

Technique: This procedure is designed to provide the student with the opportunity to earn activity or free time for increasing the number of questions correct during a reading class.

Most Likely to Benefit: This procedure will help motivate students who are unwilling to do work in reading class although they are able to read fluently. These students often do not complete reading work given in class, but when given the opportunity to earn activity time, their reading performance increases within acceptable teacher-set goals.

Materials: A Mystery Motivator worksheet, a clear-colored felt-tip marking pen (this comes with markers called Erasables), a colored marker, and a reading assignment.

Baseline: Baseline for interventions that are to increase rate of reading:

Ask the student to read three reading passages for one minute from reading material at the student's grade level. As the student reads, mark any words omitted, substituted, or mispronounced as an error. It is important to tell the student the word quickly so that they do not struggle with one word for most of the minute timing. This assessment procedure is estimating how many words the child *can read* accurately at a certain rate. Hence, if a student hesitates for more than *three seconds* with a word, tell the student the word.

Your baseline score will be the middle score from the three probes. For example, if the student read 50 words, 60 words, and 55 words, the baseline score would be 55.

or

For interventions that are to increase comprehension:

Collect and review reading worksheets that the student was required to do in class.

After collecting the student's work, determine the percent correct on the worksheets. These scores will be used as baseline scores. Students who are performing 70% or lower on most worksheets may need a motivating strategy to increase their performance. Test this possibility by asking the student to do one of the worksheets again. However, this time the student will be provided with some activity or reward if he is able to increase his score within acceptable teacher-set range or 25% higher.

If the student is able to increase his score within acceptable ranges, use the following procedure in the classroom.

Treatment Procedure:

1. Ask the student to pick out three or four activities that she would like to earn for good work during reading class. However, you should have the opportunity to preapprove each of the activities that the student selects.

2. At the beginning of the week, construct a Mystery Motivator using the clear-colored marking pen.

3. Discuss with the student a goal that is challenging yet attainable. If the student sets his goal too low, then you will need to determine a goal.

4. On the Mystery Motivator worksheet, write 0, 3, or 5 minutes in the stars. Write more 3s and 5s when first starting this procedure. This ensures that the student will earn activities quickly.

5. Place the Mystery Motivator worksheet on the student's desk during reading class.

6. When the student is given independent seat work, remind the student that she is given the chance to earn activity time for accurate work.

7. After the student completes her goal, the student will raise a hand to signal that her work is ready to be graded.

8. Correct the student's work. If the student was able to get all the problems correct, the student can color in a star on the activity time chart. If the student did not get all of the problems correct, then the missed problems can be included into the next goal. Reteach any needed steps at this time.

9. The student will write his reading score and activity time earned on a chart. The work will be kept in a student folder.

10. To further enhance reading performance, give the earned activity time as soon as possible.

Progress Monitoring:

The student's progress in the number of correct answers will be evaluated. You can expect that the student will be working toward completing all questions at 85% or above. When the student is consistently performing at about 85% correct, the student's goals may be increased. Furthermore, fill in more 0s and 3s than 5s in the stars to fade out the amount of activity time. However, provide a lot of social praise for good work to replace the activity time.

During the reading class, the student may be requiring a lot of your assistance. The student should be told that he is allowed only one or two questions during the reading time. However, if the student continues to miss many questions, an intervention, such as peer tutoring, may be needed to increase the student's reading skills.

Source:

Moore, L.A., Waguespack, A.M., Wickstrom, K.F., Witt, J.C., & Gaydos, G.G. (1994). Mystery motivator: An effective and time efficient intervention. *School Psychology, 23*, 106-118.

MYSTERY MOTIVATOR

Name: ______________________________

Date	Goal or Best Score	Words Read Correctly	Number of Errors	Meet Your Goal?

Self-Monitoring Math Problems

Technique:

Some students seem to answer math problems incorrectly; however, upon further inspection, the students may be doing some of the individual steps needed to get the correct answer while consistently missing others. This procedure provides students with continuous instructional cues or steps that help guide students as they work their math problems during independent seat work.

Most Likely to Benefit:

This procedure will help motivate students who are unwilling to do work in math class although they are able to do math problems fluently. These students often do not complete math work given in class, but when given the opportunity to earn activity time, their math performance increases within acceptable teacher-set goals.

Materials:

An individual math checklist, math assignment, and a student chart or graph.

Baseline:

Give the students math problems. Tell the students to do the problems without any help. After the students complete the work, examine the type of errors that the students are making on incorrect answers. Make a list of the errors.

Student Training:

1. Make a checklist for each student that tells the students how to correct each of the errors on the error list. A short and simple sentence telling the students what to do will be sufficient to remind the students to do the problem correctly. (See Figure 29.)

2. Show the students the checklists.

Figure 29. Example Checklist

Example Checklist

- ❑ I copied the problem correctly.
- ❑ I regrouped when I needed to (top number is bigger than bottom).
- ❑ I borrowed correctly (number crossed out is one bigger).
- ❑ I subtracted all the numbers.
- ❑ I subtracted correctly.

3. Point out the steps that they will need to review on the checklist as they work through the problem.

4. Give the students a problem to do.

5. Tell the students to put a plus sign next to each step on the checklist that was completed correctly and a minus sign next to any step that was incorrect or skipped.

6. Tell the students to raise their hands to signal that they have completed their work. Review students' checklists.

7. Tell the students that they will begin using the checklists independently in class and at home once they are able to answer several problems accurately and have placed correct marks by each of the steps.

Treatment Procedure:

1. Place the checklists on the students' desks at the beginning of math class.

2. Remind the students to use the checklists when working on problems.

3. Monitor the students working on problems and using the checklists. If a student is not using his checklist, prompt the student to look at the checklist as he works.

4. Approach the student when you notice the student raising her hand.

5. Check the student's work.

6. Praise the student for checking off the steps on the checklist.

7. If the student did not follow a step on any problem, then tell the student to redo the problem. If the student is unable to do the problem(s) correctly, help the student with the problem and tell the student to redo the problem three times.

8. Remind the students to write the number of points earned on their graph or chart.

9. To make the treatment more effective, the students can earn free time or some other activity for a certain amount of points at the end of the day or week. The students will earn one point for each correct response, and one point for each problem in which all of the steps on the checklist were self-monitored accurately.

Optional: To provide more practice for the student, give the student a checklist to complete as he is completing his homework. The student can earn additional points for accuracy and the correct recordings of a plus or minus for each problem.

Progress Monitoring: The student will write the number of points earned for each correct answer and correct self-monitoring on the checklist. When the student is able to do the work above 90% accuracy on several worksheets, remove the checklist. The student may still earn points, however, for each correct response.

Source:

Dunlap, L.K. & Dunlap, G. (1989). A self-monitoring package for teaching subtraction with regrouping to students with learning disabilities. *Journal of Applied Behavior Analysis, 22*, 309-314.

STUDENT SELF-MONITORING CHART

Name: ______________________________

Date	Number of Problems	Points for Correct Answers	Points for Correct Checklist

CHECKLIST

Name: ______________________________

Monitor these steps:	#1	#2	#3	#4	#5	#6	#7	#8	#9	#10
1.										
2.										
3.										
4.										
5.										
6.										
7.										

Star Chart

Technique: Typically, students who have a number of disruptive off-task behaviors are not completing their work. Frequently, these students may be more motivated to get peer or teacher attention than to pay attention and to work in class. This type of intervention would be implemented to provide the child with immediate feedback, potent reinforcement for accurate work completion, and systematic progress monitoring. The teacher will provide the child with systematic attention for accurate class work and on-task behaviors. Furthermore, the child will not be allowed to avoid the work that he is capable of completing.

Most likely to benefit: Students who are able to do the work, but are not completing their class work are most likely to benefit from this procedure. For example, a student may be misbehaving above 30% of the time and averaging less than 70% on class work. However, this student performance increases above 70% when given the chance to earn a reward for accurate work.

Materials: A Star Chart worksheet, Things I Would Like to Earn list (see example), and work assignments.

Baseline: Assess both the student's behavior and academic performance. First, conduct a behavioral observation of the student during a subject where she has the most frequent behavior problems. For the academic baseline performance, collect the work during the observations and any work that has been collected from the past few weeks. If the work performance is low (below 15% per week) and misbehavior is high (i.e., above 30% disruptive behavior), determine small behavior goals within a subject period. For example, the student needs to complete four problems correctly before earning a star.

Student Training: This student will need to have strong motivators in place in order to work appropriately. There are several ways to assess what types of motivators will work for a particular student. First, observe what activities the student prefers during free time. Second, develop an Activity Survey list of several activities from which the student can choose (see example). Finally, ask the student to pick out four activities from the activity list that he would be willing to work for in class.

Organize a chart for the student to place on his desk so that he can keep track of his stars (see example). Tell the student that stars will be earned for a certain amount of accurate work. In addition, tell the student that a star will be taken away each time he is off task (e.g., talking, touching others, not looking at his paper, etc.).

Each star will represent 30 seconds of activity time. During activity time, the student can pick an activity and/or a partner to play with from a list of three or four predetermined activities. After every subject, the student will write down how many stars he has on his chart.

The student will need to be trained to work quietly, to raise her hand quietly when the work is complete, and shown how to fill out a star chart.

Treatment Procedure:

1. Place the star chart on the student's desk at the beginning of the day. The student will start with five stars.

2. Remind the student that she will be able to earn additional stars for a certain amount of problems that are completed accurately. Also remind the student that she may lose these five stars for off-task behavior.

3. When the student is given work, place a mark after a certain number of problems that should be completed by the student in a short amount of time.

4. The student will work quietly on the problems up to that mark. When he has completed the problems, he will quietly raise his hand and wait for you to come and grade his work. If the student does not complete the work in the time allotted, he will be required to do the work after school, during recess, or during free time.

5. Grade the student's work. If the work is accurate, praise the student for his good work and circle or initial a star on the chart.

6. Then draw a new line for the next set of problems that the student will need to work on. However, if the work is incorrect, then reteach the needed steps and tell the student to raise her hand again after she has tried to correct the problem(s).

7. The student will also calculate the percent correct and write it on the Star Chart.

8. The stars earned by the student will then be exchanged for activity time. Activity time can be given both in the morning and afternoon depending on what is more effective for the student.

9. Mark an X over the first star if the student is off task (e.g., talking, touching others, not looking at his paper, etc.). If the student reacts inappropriately, place an X over a second star. If the student reacts inappropriately a second time, the student will see the principal.

Progress Monitoring:

There are several outcomes that would be expected if this intervention was implemented. First, the student would be expected to be able to complete more problems accurately. To that end, the student's work will be collected in order to determine if the number of problems completed accurately has increased. Improvement should be seen within one week. Second, if the student is able to do the work and is motivated by the reinforcers, then the student should be able to earn a certain amount of stars per day for good work and behavior. The amount of expected stars to be earned per week will be determined directly from observations in the classroom and upon review of the student's work before the intervention was implemented.

Source:

Shapiro, E.S. & Goldberg, R. (1986). A comparison of group contingencies for increasing spelling performance among sixth-grade students. *School Psychology Review, 15*, 546-557.

THINGS I WOULD LIKE TO EARN

____ 1. Library time

____ 2. Fun reading time

____ 3. Playing board games (checkers, connect four, etc.)

____ 4. Puzzle time

____ 5. Art time

____ 6. Coloring

____ 7. Computer time

____ 8. Clean chalk board or eraser

____ 9. Run an errand

____10. Tutor other students

____11. Play table games (tic-tac-toe, hangman)

____12. Choose the class story during story time

____13. Share a story with a teacher or the class

____14. Pick up papers for teacher

____15. Help teacher organize materials for the class

____16. Hand out materials to students during class

____17. Call out answers during grading

____18. Pick a group to work with

____19. Sit and work with a friend

____20. Grade papers

____21. Make announcements over loudspeaker

____22. Phone parent to say hello

____23. Five minute nap

____24. Sit in another class

____25. Helping in the library

____26. Helping the janitor

____27. Sitting next to the teacher at lunch

____28. Have lunch with the principal

____29. Sitting near teacher's desk for a work assignment

____30. Write in journal

____31. Pick the student who helps the teacher

____32. Earn free time/activity time minutes for class

____33. Clean cafeteria tables

____34. Pick your place in line

____35. Pick where you sit during a work assignment

____36. Post good work in class

____37. Hug from the teacher

____38, Be a team captain or leader

____39. Show work to another class or to the principal

____40. Lead class in a class activity such as pledge of allegiance

____41. Decorate bulletin board

____42. Sharpen class pencils

____43. Write work directions or homework on board

STAR CHART

Name: ____________________

	Subject	Goal	Number of Stars Earned	Behavior Rating	Goal Met?
Monday	Reading			☺ 😐 ☹	
	Spelling			☺ 😐 ☹	
	English			☺ 😐 ☹	
	Math			☺ 😐 ☹	
				☺ 😐 ☹	
Tuesday	Reading			☺ 😐 ☹	
	Spelling			☺ 😐 ☹	
	English			☺ 😐 ☹	
	Math			☺ 😐 ☹	
				☺ 😐 ☹	
Wednesday	Reading			☺ 😐 ☹	
	Spelling			☺ 😐 ☹	
	English			☺ 😐 ☹	
	Math			☺ 😐 ☹	
				☺ 😐 ☹	
Thursday	Reading			☺ 😐 ☹	
	Spelling			☺ 😐 ☹	
	English			☺ 😐 ☹	
	Math			☺ 😐 ☹	
				☺ 😐 ☹	
Friday	Reading			☺ 😐 ☹	
	Spelling			☺ 😐 ☹	
	English			☺ 😐 ☹	
	Math			☺ 😐 ☹	

Helping the Class Improve Spelling Scores

Technique:

Many students have difficulty studying spelling words on their own or getting extra practice at home. However, students can help each other practice their words in class for a few minutes a day. The entire class can then be rewarded for their efforts if they meet a teacher-set spelling performance goal at the end of the week.

Most Likely to Benefit:

Students who are able to learn spelling words with some practice but need additional motivation to maintain adequate levels of spelling performance are most likely to benefit from this procedure. For example, a student may be averaging below 70% on the spelling tests but will be able to get above 70% when told she will earn a reward for accurate spelling performance. Although one student may need this additional motivation to adequately perform, this strategy promotes better spelling performance for the entire class.

Materials:

Spelling words and a Good Job jar. Write preferred activities on slips of paper, fold the papers, and then put the papers in the Good Job jar.

Baseline:

Both the class average and individual student progress can be monitored in this intervention. Calculate the class average for the last three end-of-the-week spelling tests. If there is a specific individual that needs to be monitored, that student's last three spelling tests scores will be his baseline performance.

Treatment Procedure:

1. Before introducing spelling words at the beginning of the week, inform the students that the class will be working together to earn Good Job time for spelling test scores at the end of the week. The class will earn some reward if the class is able to get 90% or better on the spelling test.

2. Brainstorm with the class on various activities or prizes that they would be willing to earn.

3. Have several students write the ideas on small pieces of paper. The students can fold the papers and put them into a Good Job jar.

4. Organize study groups or partners. Designate 5 to 10 minutes each school day for the students to work with each other to learn the spelling words.

5. During practice time, set a timer for 3 to 5 minutes.

6. One student will read the words to her partner while the partner writes the words. When the timer rings, the students switch roles. If there are students who have difficulty reading the words, use groups of three. These students can also practice the test two times before reading the words out loud to their partners.

7. The students can grade the words after the practice session.

8. Teach spelling lessons as usual throughout the week.

9. On Thursday, remind students about the Good Job reward. Pick an activity from the Good Job jar.

10. On Friday, give and grade the spelling tests.

11. Determine if the students have earned the Good Job reward. If the class did not meet the goal, encourage the students to try harder next week.

Progress Monitoring:

Each student's progress on the weekly spelling test will be evaluated. Due to the additional practice provided during class time, student's individual scores should increase. If certain students' scores are not increasing or are not within acceptable levels, these students may need additional practice. Interventions such as the Write/Say method can easily be implemented while the teacher continues to use this procedure for the rest of the class.

Sources:

Delquadri, J.C., Greenwood, C.R., Stretton, K., & Hall, R.V. (1983). The peer tutoring spelling game: A classroom procedure for increasing opportunity to respond and spelling performance. *Education and Treatment of Children, 6,* 225-239.

Shapiro, E.S. & Goldberg, R. (1986). A comparison of group contingencies for increasing spelling performance among sixth-grade students. *School Psychology Review, 15,* 546-557.

IMPROVEMENT IN SPELLING CHART

Name: ______________________________

Date of Spelling Test	Student or Class Average	Activity Earned

My Time May Be Your Time

Technique: This procedure is designated to maintain the time allotted to academic instruction. Students are able to earn free time after they have put in a hard day's work. However, students will lose their free time if they disrupt the teacher's planned academic time.

Most Likely to Benefit: This procedure is particularly useful for classrooms that have frequent amounts of disruptive behavior during academic instruction and transition times of longer than four minutes when moving from one activity to the next. That is, there is 30% or more of the off-task behavior occurring during transitions and/or instructional time.

Materials: Two timers

Baseline: Observe the classroom and determine the percentage of disruptive behavior and off-task behavior that occurs. Randomly pick different students to evaluate during 10-second intervals. Time the transitions where the students are directed into another activity and the time they actually begin the new activity.

Treatment Procedure:

1. Determine the amount of time students need to complete work or follow directions.

2. Give the students any needed directions.

3. Tell the students the amount of time in which they are required to prepare for an academic lesson or to complete work.

4. Explain to the students that you will set the timer for that amount of time and stop the timer whenever a student is not working or following directions. This will be the Good Work timer.

5. However, a second timer will also be set. This timer will include extra free time the students may earn.

6. If the Good Work timer goes off before the Free Time timer, then the class earns the amount of time left on the Free Time timer during a set free time period. The free time period may be both in the morning and in the afternoon.

7. Set the timers and tell students to begin.

8. If a student is off task, stop and hold up the Good Work timer.

9. Tell the misbehaving student what they should be doing in a voice that the entire class can hear.

10. If the student does not comply, warn the student that the Good Work timer is stopped and free time is being lost.

11. When the student complies, restart the Good Work timer.

12. To make this intervention work, make sure that the students get their free time as planned.

Progress Monitoring: Teachers should expect that students are earning some or all of the available free time.

Problem Solving: If one or several students are sabotaging the free time for the class, then they may need to be put on a separate contingence.

Source:

Cowen, R.J., Jones, F.H., & Bellack, A.S. (1979). Grandma's Rule with group contingencies: A cost-effective means of classroom management. *Behavior Modification*, *3*, 397-418.

CHAPTER 5

Intervention and Teaching Strategies When: The Student Needs More Practice

If your assessment has indicated that the student simply needs to spend more time practicing the material, there are many options available. Generally, students who need more practice perform a skill in a relatively accurate manner but are not fluent. Practice helps these students to develop fluency and to become more automatic in their responding. This chapter offers some general as well as some specific strategies for improving fluency.

General Strategies for the Student Who Needs More Practice

Increase the Time Available for Practice

A simple and direct way of increasing practice time is to increase the time allocated for practice. For example, a teacher schedules 40 minutes daily for math, and perhaps half of that time is set aside for instruction and half is designated for practice. If most students can already accurately perform the skill but many do so at a low fluency level, then it makes sense to reallocate some of the time allotted from instruction to practice. Teaching builds accuracy, but practice builds fluency.

If this reallocation of instruction time is not possible, there is nothing that says you can't offer practice times throughout the day. This actually may prove more effective since some students will not have the attention spans to complete five skill sheets in one sitting. But students are able to complete three to five skill sheets a day if the practice times are throughout the day.

Change the Learning Channel

Some students perform much more slowly when working in one Learning Channel versus another. Sometimes just changing from See/Write to See/Say can improve students' performance considerably.

Use Flash Cards

Flash cards can be used, especially for sight word vocabulary in reading and for math facts. As you go through the deck of flash cards with the student, corrects are placed in one pile and incorrects are placed in another pile. The student is required to reattempt those in the incorrect pile at least once. You can also practice pacing the student by showing the flash card for only about a second. The student must respond in that amount of time or the next card is presented. This is a way to provide a prompt for increasing speed. Students can also practice with flash cards on their own.

Flash card software programs are also available. Some students will be more motivated to practice if a computer is used. Some of these computer programs allow you to build your own "decks," which makes the task easier for the teacher.

Peer Tutoring

The drawback with flash cards and some other types of practice opportunities is that usually you must administer and score them. Peer tutoring is a way that two students can help each other without demanding too much of your time. All the students need are some extra skill sheets or some flash cards with answers on the back and a little training in how to perform the task. It is also good to remind them of your expectations for their behavior during peer tutoring.

SPECIFIC VALIDATED PRACTICES FOR STUDENTS WHO NEED MORE PRACTICE

Drill and Overcorrection to Improve Reading

Technique: While extra practice has proven to be effective in increasing reading fluency, an error correction procedure greatly reduces the number of reading errors. This procedure is designed to provide students with reading practice, immediate feedback on errors, and direct rehearsal of error corrections before trying to improve a reading score.

Most Likely to Benefit: Some students need the extra practice if they are making a large number of errors (e.g., 5 errors per minute). If a student is not improving her score after listening to a passage, then she may need the extra practice provided in this procedure.

Materials: Each reading passage should be approximately 200 words. Other needed materials are a timer, a pencil, and a chart or graph.

Baseline: Ask the student to read three reading passages for one minute from reading material at the student's grade level. As the student reads, mark any words omitted, substituted, or mispronounced as an error. It is important to tell the student the word quickly so that he does not struggle with one word for most of the one-minute timing. This assessment procedure is estimating how many words the student *can read* accurately at a certain rate. Hence, if a student hesitates more than *three seconds* with a word, tell the student the word.

The student's baseline score will be the median score from the three reading probes. The goal is to determine the appropriate grade level of reading material for instruction. The student should be able to read at a rate within a certain range of words per minute depending on their grade level. Refer to Table 6 for the appropriate range of reading rates for the student.

Table 6. Appropriate Reading Rates

Student's Grade Level	The Student's Instructional Reading Range
1st, 2nd, or 3rd	40 to 60 words per minute
4th or above	70 to 100 words per minute

First assess the student on reading materials appropriate for his or her grade level. If the student is reading below the instructional range, assess the student on reading materials at one lower grade level. Keep assessing the student one lower grade level until the student is able to read within the instructional range.

Treatment Procedure:

1. Ask the student to practice reading a passage out loud.

2. Stop the student whenever a word is omitted, substituted, mispronounced, or the student cannot read the word.

3. Tell the student the missed word. Ask the student to say the missed word correctly five times.

4. Praise the student by saying, "That's right! That word is _____" if the student says the word correctly.

5. Tell the student to continue reading starting with the sentence containing the missed word.

6. Tell the student to continue reading the passage.

7. Continue to correct the student if he or she missed a word, ask the student to say the word five times, and repeat the sentence containing the missed word as the student continues to read the passage.

8. Tell the student to reread the entire passage for one minute.

9. Set the timer for one minute.

10. Start the timer and tell the student to begin reading.

11. Say the word for the student if the student hesitates more than three seconds with a word.

12. Draw a line through any word that was misread.

13. Mark the last word read after one minute.

14. Count the number of words read correctly and mark the number on a chart or graph. The teacher should praise the student for his or her score and hard work.

Progress Monitoring: The number of words read correctly and the number of errors made in the one-minute timed reading are to be recorded. Teachers should expect that students' number of errors will decrease to one or two mistakes while words correct will steadily increase (i.e., 60 words for 1st and 2nd grade and 100 for greater than 3rd grade per minute).

Sources:

Singh, N.N. (1990). Effects of two error-correction procedures on oral reading errors: Word supply versus sentence repeat. *Behavior Modification, 14*, 188-199.

Singh, N.N. & Singh, J. (1986). A behavioral remediation program for oral reading: Effects on errors and comprehension. *Educational Psychology, 6*(2), 105-114.

READING PRACTICE & GOALS CHART

Name: ______________________________

Date	Goal or Best Score	Words Read Correctly	Number of Errors	Met Goal?

Saying and Writing Spelling Words Accurately

Technique: This procedure promotes spelling accuracy on weekly spelling tests by providing students with directed rehearsal of unknown spelling words. Moreover, this procedure teaches students to sound out words as they try to spell unknown words correctly.

Most Likely to Benefit: This procedure is most helpful for students who are consistently getting below 70% correct on weekly spelling tests and who are reading below 20 words per minute on grade level reading passages.

Materials: Weekly spelling tests.

Baseline: Collect the results of the last five weekly spelling tests.

Treatment Procedure: There are several ways to conduct this procedure in the classroom. For example, you can work with an individual student or a small group of students. Or a peer tutor can easily be trained to carry out the following steps.

Monday

1. Give students the list of spelling words.

2. Say the words out loud for the students.

3. Tell students to study the words on their own.

Tuesday

4. Give students a pretest by saying each of the words out loud to the students and having the students write the words.

5. Grade the tests.

6. Circle the misspelled part of each word to highlight the type of error made.

7. For every incorrect word on the pretest, tell the students to say and write each word correctly *five* times. You or a peer tutor can give and grade pretests with a small group of students.

8. Review the rewritten words.

Wednesday

9. Give a second spelling pretest.

10. Grade the tests.

11. Circle the misspelled parts of each word to highlight the type of errors made.

12. For every incorrect word on the test, tell the students to *say* and *write* each word correctly *10* times.

13. Review the rewritten words.

Thursday

14. Give a third spelling pretest.

15. Grade the tests.

16. Circle the misspelled part of each word to highlight the type of errors made.

17. For every incorrect word on the test, tell the students to say and write each word correctly 15 times.

18. Review the rewritten words.

Friday

19. Give the final spelling test to assess for spelling accuracy.

20. Praise the students for correct spelling words.

Progress Monitoring:

Place the student's pretests and spelling tests in a folder. At the end of each session, have the student record the number of errors made on each test. You can expect an improvement in the student's performance as the week progresses. When a student has performed at or above 90% correct on two or more consecutive Friday tests, the sessions may be sliced back to two sessions on Wednesday and Thursday. However, continue to monitor the student's scores to determine if the student is able to maintain adequate performance.

Source:

Kearney, C.A. & Drabman, R.S. (1993). The write-say method for improving spelling accuracy in children with learning disabilities. *Journal of Learning Disabilities*, *26*, 52-55.

SPELLING CHART

Student Name: ______________________________

Date of Spelling Test	Spelling Test Score	Date of Spelling Test	Spelling Test Score

Increasing Writing Fluency Performance

Technique:

Students are often able to *tell* a story but have difficulty *writing* the story on paper. Moreover, writing for some students may be slow and awkward. With practice, however, students can learn to write their ideas on paper more rapidly. This strategy provides students with frequent practice opportunities and writing goals to work toward.

Most Likely to Benefit:

Students who are writing below the average words per minute.

Materials:

Story starters, writing journals, writing charts or graphs, and a timer.

Baseline:

Assess the students using a story starter. Tell the students that they will write a story. Give the students a story starter and one minute to think about what they want to write. Set a timer for three minutes and tell the students to begin writing. Review each student's story and count the number of words that you are able to read. Hence, even misspelled words count if you can read them.

Treatment Procedure:

1. Set a designated time for students to write each day. For example, immediately in the morning, after recess, or after lunch.

2. Tell the students that their journals should be on their desks but remained closed until you tell them to begin writing.

3. Tell students that they will be writing for 10 minutes each day. (This time may be shorter for younger children. However, the time should be consistent from day to day.)

4. Tell the students a story starter that they can use to begin thinking about a story to write about for 10 minutes.

5. Give the students one or two minutes to think about what they are going to write about.

6. Set a timer for 10 minutes and tell the students to begin writing.

7. After the 10 minutes has passed, tell the students to close their journals.

8. Tell the students to count all of the words that they have written.

9. Instruct students to write the number of words that they have written on a chart or plot the number on a graph.

10. Students enjoy trying to beat their best scores or reaching certain goals. Moreover, students can be rewarded for their progress. For example, students can earn activity time for reaching 500 words, the class earns activity time for a total of 5,000 words, or the class earns activity time if everyone meets the teacher-set goal.

Progress Monitoring:

While students are writing, check one-third of the students' charts or graphs. You should expect that students will increase the amount of words that are written over time. However, students will peak at some maximum number, depending upon how much each individual is capable of writing any amount of letters in that time. Other goals can also be attained as students improve, such as number of transitions, sentences, proper capitalization, or punctuation.

Source:

Moxley, R.A., Lutz, P.A., Ahlhorn, P., Boley, N., & Armstrong, L. (1995). Self-recorded word counts of free-writing in grades 1-4. *Education and Treatment of Children, 18*, 138-157.

WRITING PERFORMANCE CHART

Name: ______________________________

Date	Writing Time	Goal	Number of Words Written Correctly	Points Earned

CHAPTER 6

Intervention and Teaching Strategies When:

The Student Needs More Help

This chapter provides strategies for students who need more help or assistance to do the work. While the previous chapter was for students who were accurate but not fluent, these strategies are designed for students who are not even accurate in the first place. We will again begin with some general ideas and strategies for providing various types of help. This will be followed by a section on specific research-validated practices.

General Strategies for the Student Who Needs More Help

Teach the Skill Systematically

For students who are having difficulty accurately performing the skill, we recommend teaching the skill very thoroughly as a beginning point. One technique for the "tough" learner is a procedure we call "Nuclear Teaching." Nuclear Teaching is a powerful tool because it incorporates several proven methods of providing help, including modeling and feedback. Figure 30 describes how to use Nuclear Teaching methods with the currently assigned *Basic Skill Builders* sheet.

Figure 30. Nuclear Teaching

Step

1: Model the skill.

Tell the student, "I will do it first to show you how."
Use the student's currently assigned skill sheet.
If the subject is reading, read for approximately one minute.

If the subject is math, complete problems for one minute as you talk aloud the steps involved.

For some students, you can also model self-reinforcement. At the end of your performance, give yourself a pat on the back by saying, "Good job."

Step 2: Perform the skill with the student.

Tell the student, "I am going to do it with you."

The idea is to let the student do as much of it as he is capable of doing. However, without any hesitation, you will help the student perform the skill if he has any hesitation.

You can help by giving hints, directing the student to the next step, or reminding the student of any forgotten steps.

Step 3: Ask the student to perform the skill while you watch and provide feedback.

Say to the student, "Now it is your turn to try it by yourself."

Have the student practice the same skill sheet while you watch and provide feedback. You should use the very same reading passage, math problems, etc., that you have just practiced with the student.

In reading, for example, you would allow the student to read the passage you modeled and helped the student to read and, if the student does not know one of the words, you tell the student the word after a brief pause. In math, if the answer is wrong, immediately provide feedback to that effect. With this step, in contrast to Step 2, the student performs the skill more independently.

Step 4: Conduct daily one-minute timings using skill sheets.

Step 5: Allow the student to complete the skill sheet without any assistance. Record this performance on the chart as the score for the day.

Prompting

A prompt is a detail or a cue that is added which makes learning and remembering a skill easier for students. Some students, for example, have difficulty remembering the difference between a "b" and a "d." A creative teacher somewhere came up with an ingenious prompt to help children remember that difference:

Figure 31. Prompt for "b" and "d" difference

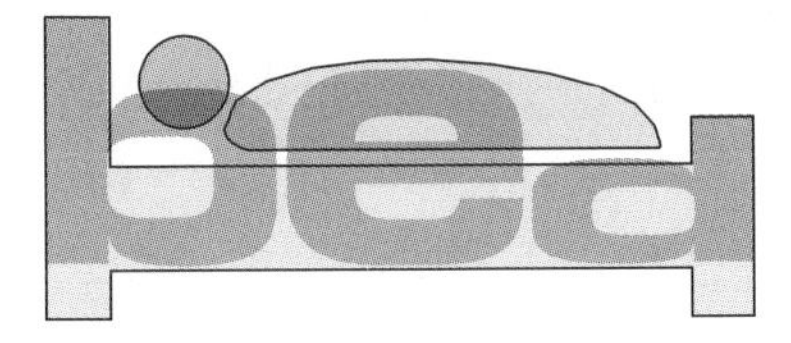

Whenever the student needs to know a "b" from a "d," he can simply make a "bed" which provides a visual prompt for the difference. In the South, a prompt for the symbol greater than (i.e., >) is that it resembles an alligator's mouth (in the West, it is the shark's mouth), and the alligator's mouth points to the larger object because the alligator always wants to eat the larger thing.

Most prompting in schools occurs when another person (i.e., peer or teacher) provides a prompt in the form of a hint or by pointing to the correct answer. Those teachers who have asked students to think about what a math sign (e.g., plus or minus) is asking the students to do have provided a prompt. Some reading programs provide prompts by initially leaving the lines above the vowels to indicate whether the specific vowel is long or short. A prompt, then, is just a little something extra to help the student perform correctly. The prompt can be gradually faded out when the student can perform the skill more independently.

Modeling

"Modeling" refers to a demonstration of the skill prior to a student's performance. In reading, Listening Passage Preview is an instructional technique that has been shown by research to improve reading. It is a modeling technique because it involves the teacher (or someone else) reading the passage aloud before the student reads it.

Many students can learn skills quickly through modeling because *seeing* the skill performed makes it easier to duplicate the skill rather than just listening to an explanation of *how to* perform the skill. Many adults, for example, might have difficulty following an explanation of how to do long division, but they could more quickly grasp the concept if they saw someone compute several long division problems.

More Frequent Feedback

When using skill sheets, a student would normally receive feedback after each performance by counting the number correct. Some students require feedback more frequently when they are first learning a skill. The feedback may provide information about whether they are correct or incorrect. In addition, the feedback may simply provide encouragement for attempting the work or continuing to work for longer periods of time.

As a child, you may have played the game where someone hides something and you are supposed to find it. You are given feedback in terms of "warmer" or "colder" as to whether you are getting closer or farther from the object. Some students *need* this same type of feedback to guide them to make correct responses or to merely continue working.

SPECIFIC VALIDATED PRACTICES FOR STUDENTS WHO NEED MORE HELP

Response Cards for Increasing Letter and Letter-Sound Identification

Technique:

Reading begins with the development of linking the sounds of the letters to units in the written language, or in other words, increasing phonemic awareness. Furthermore, the amount of time that students engage in instruction on phonics is found to be a strong predictor of their reading achievement (Adams, 1990). In the classroom, teachers often provide practice opportunities by listening to a group of students practice their sounds by verbally sounding out letters. However, it is difficult to determine if all of the students have mastered the skill. With the use of response cards, teachers can quickly determine individual progress while working with a large group of students.

Response cards are cards or signs that a student holds up to show an answer to a teacher question. For example, the teacher can ask the students to show or write the letter for the sound "buh." This procedure effectively increases the number of opportunities that a student has to academically respond. Furthermore, the teacher can quickly monitor which students comprehend the lesson.

Most Likely to Benefit:

This procedure will increase performance for students that make a large number of reading errors or pronounce letters below 40 letters per minute. However, this intervention will benefit all students learning letters and sounds.

Materials:

Charts or graphs, blank cards or pieces of paper, small chalkboards or white laminated boards, and a timer. Each student can also make response cards for each alphabet letter.

Baseline:

There are two baseline measures for this procedure. Count the number of times a student responds to questions during a reading class or assess the student's rate on identifying letters and saying their phonetic sound. Tell the students that they will be saying as many letters as they can within one minute. Set and start a timer for one minute. Tell the student to begin saying each of the letters. If the student gets stuck on a letter, tell the student the letter after a 3 second delay. Mark any letter omitted or substituted as an error. Calculate the number of letters the student said correctly. The same procedure can be repeated with the student sounding out each of the letters.

Figure 32. Examples of Reading Errors

- **Word Substitution:**

  "dog" for "cat."

- **Mispronunciation:**

  "dig" for "dog."

- **Omission of a word or a line of words.**

Student Training: Initially, the students should be shown how to use the cards and have an opportunity to practice with easy, fun questions. The teacher should also provide the students with a clear signal that tells students when to hold up a card or put a card down. The students will learn from others, so monitoring for cheating is not necessary.

Treatment Procedure:

1. Tell the students to place their letter cards on their desks.

2. Tell the students that they will hold up the letter that you call out.

3. Feedback should be provided based on the majority of responses presented to the teacher. Provide feedback by saying, "Most of you know that letter!" If there are a number of errors, the teacher may ask the question again after giving some additional cues or prompts. Say, "The 'A' looks like this letter" and hold up the correct letter. Have the students try the letter again.

4. Continue this process until all letters in the lesson are covered. If the students are missing certain letters, repeat these several times until they are able to pick those letters accurately within three to five seconds.

5. Say the letters at a fairly rapid pace to maintain student attention.

6. This procedure can also be done with the identification of phonetic sounds. Ask the students to hold up a card for each sound.

7. Assess individual students daily if several students are working on this skill. Tell the students that they will be saying as many letters as they can within one minute. Set and start a timer for one minute. Have one of the students begin saying each of the letters. If the student gets stuck on a letter, tell the student the letter after a three second delay. Mark any letter omitted or substituted as an error. Calculate the number of letters the student said correctly. The same procedure can be repeated with the student sounding out each of the letters. Repeat one-minute timing for each student needing help with this skill.

8. Write the number of letters that the student correctly identified on the student's chart. The student can also earn points or free time for beating his best score.

Once the students have mastered identifying sounds with letters, there are several phonic awareness skills that can be taught also using the response cards.

a. Identifying sounds in words.

   Say a word slowly and try to "stretch" the word. Tell the student to write or pick a letter card that represents the beginning and end sound of the word. Stop consonants are introduced first (i.e., b, d, g, k, p, and t).

b. Phenome counting.

   Say a word slowly. Tell the student to tap out the sounds and write the number of sounds in the word on a response card. Begin with two phenome segments, then progress to three, and then four.

c. Phenome blending.

   Say individual sounds. For example, ask, "What word would we have if you put these sounds together: /s/, /a/, /t/?" Ask students to write the word on a response card. If errors are made, have the students correct the spelling. Irregular words should be avoided at this stage.

d. Word to word matching. For example, "Do 'pen' and 'pip' begin with the same letter?"

e. Odd word out. For example, "What word starts with a different sound: 'bag,' 'nine,' 'beach,' and 'bike'?" This can be done orally or as a written assignment.

Progress Monitoring: As the students present the response cards, scan students' responses. Note students who may need additional practice if they are frequently writing or picking the incorrect response. These students may need to be further assessed individually by following Step 7. If these students are performing at 35 letters or less (or 25 letters or more below the upper class scores), then peer tutoring may be needed. Alternatively, the students could use an audiotape and listen to a taped preview of the story.

Optional:

1. Response cards can also be used for individual interventions. For example, a peer can ask questions or pick out words for the student to practice in a peer tutoring session. The peer can monitor the number of correct answers, or, preferably, the tutee can write the answers on different cards to make progress monitoring easier for the teacher. The peer tutor can also write down the answers, so the two students can keep track of the number of correct matches throughout the session.

2. During the lesson, the student can place her correct answers in one pile and incorrect answers in another pile. The incorrect cards can then be used for the student to study or practice at home.

Source:

Narayan, J.S., Heward, W.L., Gardner, R., III, Courson, F.H., & Omness, C.K. (1990). Using response cards to increase student participation in an elementary classroom. *Journal of Applied Behavior Analysis*, *23* (4), 483-490.

Name: ______________________________

PROGRESS CHART

Date	Number of Correct Letters	Number of Errors	Goal

Comprehension Instruction During Reading: Story Grammar or Narrative Literature

Technique: When students are learning to read faster and more accurately, they often have trouble with comprehension. However, many stories in a reading book often follow a consistent organization or structure. Students can be taught to notice this structure and use the structure to better understand the written story. A predetermined pattern of questions can be used to help students pay attention to the main ideas or structure of the stories that are commonly presented in their reading books.

Most Likely to Benefit: Students that are fluently reading material (above 70-100 words per minute) but have difficulty explaining the main ideas in a story. These students may need help in getting meaning from the text.

Materials: A narrative story with four or more basic questions.

Baseline: Before introducing the procedure, ask the student to read a story. The story should be read in the same manner that the student will read stories in class. After the student has read the story, tell the student to write the answers to four questions on her worksheet.

Treatment Procedure:

1. Model the story questions to the student.

    a. Pick a story to read with the student.

    b. Tell the student that he will be answering the four questions during the story.

    c. Tell the student to read the story aloud.

    d. Interrupt at an appropriate part in the story to ask one of the four questions.

e. Tell the student the correct answer if the student is incorrect.

f. Ask the student to summarize the answers to the four questions at the end of the story.

2. Tell the student to read a story independently after the student is able to correctly answer the questions while reading the story with the prompts.

3. Remind the student to ask herself the four questions as she reads. (See the Comprehension Coach following this activity.)

4. Tell the student to write the answers to the four questions after reading the story.

5. Remind the student to check the answers by referring back to the parts of the story that provided the answers.

6. Grade the answers.

7. If some answers are incorrect, have the student find and read aloud the relevant part of the story to prompt a correct answer.

8. Include additional questions, if needed, that require greater detail and inferences from the story once the student is consistently able to answer the four questions correctly at the end of a story.

Progress Monitoring:

The student's percentage of correct answers can be monitored throughout the course of the intervention. The percentage of correct answers to the four questions then can be charted or graphed.

Teachers should expect that students will be able to maintain an accuracy score of 75% or more on comprehension questions. If not, the student may be reading at a level that is too difficult for the student to adequately understand the reading material.

Sources:

Adams, M. *Beginning to read: Thinking & learning about print*. Cambridge, MA: MIT Press.

Grossen, B. & Carnine E. (1991). Strategies for maximizing reading success in the regular classroom. In Stoner (Ed.), *Interventions for Achievement and Behavior Problems* (p. 181-198). Washington, DC: National Association of School Psychologists.

Smith, A.M. & Van Biervliet, A. (1986). Enhancing reading comprehension through the use of a self-instructional package. *Education and Treatment of Children*, *9*, 40-55.

Student: ______________________________

COMPREHENSION COACH

(To be given to student or read to student)

Review the following four questions.

Think about the questions as you read the story.

Answer the four questions after you have read the story.

1. Who is the story about?

2. What problem does he or she have?

3. How does he or she try to fix the problem?

4. What happens at the end?

TEACHER COMPREHENSION CHECKLIST

Student:______________________________ Date:______________

Goal:____

	Mon	Tues	Wed	Thurs	Fri
Who is the story about?					
What problem does he or she have?					
How does he or she try to fix the problem?					
What happens at the end?					
Other					
Total Correct					

Improving On-Task Behavior and Reading Comprehension

Technique: This technique assists students who are able to read the material but are unable to clearly retell the story. These students often easily give up doing the work without seeking teacher assistance. Instead of requesting help, these students may work on nonacademic activities or misbehave. This intervention teaches the student how to get help from the teacher who then directs the student to key points in the reading.

Most Likely to Benefit: This procedure targets students who have difficulty explaining the information presented in the text but seldom request help. When assessed, these students are able to read the material within instructional range, but need help in learning how to recognize key points in a story that they are reading. When given questions about the information in the story, these students may be performing at 70% or lower. In the classroom, they may be on-task less than 60% of the time and ask few or no questions.

Materials: The student can be given any reading assignment. Decide on an appropriate signal for the student to succeed in getting your attention. The student can keep a chart on his desk to keep track of his help requests.

Baseline: To establish the student performance before the intervention is implemented, record how many times the student requests help during several reading assignments and the student's on-task performance. If possible, have the student answer three to five questions about the story. Score the student's answers.

Student Training: Before the intervention is used in the classroom, teach the student a signal that will be used to get your attention. For example, the student can quietly raise his hand, place a "please help" sign on his desk, or place a red cup on his desk as a signal for help. The student may need practice in thinking of the types of questions that may need to be asked. For instance, the student may need to ask about an unknown word or about information in a sentence or paragraph. Finally, show the student the Tracking Chart and have him or her practice filling out the chart correctly.

Figure 33. Examples of possible questions

- What does this word mean?
- What is the problem in the story?
- What was the order of the events in the story?
- What happened to the main character?
- What are they trying to explain in this sentence or paragraph?

Treatment Procedure:

1. Instruct the student to use the signal prior to any reading assignment.

2. Approach the student after you notice the signal and answer the question.

3. If the student is signaling inappropriately, tell the student to use the correct signal and return only when the correct signal is used.

4. Initially, you may need to approach the student during the reading assignment to prompt the child to ask a question about the reading.

Progress Monitoring:

You should expect the student to ask two to three questions per reading. Furthermore, the student should increase on-task behavior to above 70% and increase her accuracy to 80% or higher with comprehension questions given to the student after the reading. With your help, the student will learn how to ask questions that will help him to understand the reading. Furthermore, the student will learn how to pay attention to key points in a story. Hence, the student may not need to ask for help as often over time.

Reading assignments or comprehension questions may also indicate the student's understanding of the readings. If there are reading assignment or comprehension questions pertaining to the reading, grade the assignments and keep them in a folder. The student's percentage grade can be graphed and monitored. If the student is able to maintain 80% or better on comprehension questions, then gradually decrease the number of prompts given to the student.

Optional: The student may also be allowed to ask a reading partner for help three times during the reading session. If both students are unable to answer the question, then they can signal for your help.

Source:

Knapzyk, D.R. & Livingston, G. (1974). The effects of prompting question-asking upon on-task behavior and reading comprehension. *Journal of Applied Behavior Analysis*, *7*, 115-121.

TRACKING CHART

Student: ______________________________

Subjects: ______________________________

Goal for number of questions asked: ______________________________

Goal for comprehension questions: ______________________________

Subject	Number of Questions Asked	On-Task	Comprehension Questions
		☺ 😐 ☹	
		☺ 😐 ☹	
		☺ 😐 ☹	
		☺ 😐 ☹	
		☺ 😐 ☹	
		☺ 😐 ☹	
		☺ 😐 ☹	
		☺ 😐 ☹	
		☺ 😐 ☹	
		☺ 😐 ☹	
		☺ 😐 ☹	
		☺ 😐 ☹	

Peer Tutoring

Technique: Peer tutoring is a popular practice in the classroom. This approach increases the opportunities for students to practice and respond. While the students are working together, the teacher is available for frequent and immediate feedback on student progress.

Most Likely to Benefit: This approach can be used to improve reading skills for diverse learners or students with disabilities as well as the general education population.

Materials: Reading passages with a written assignment or a progress chart.

Baseline: Before beginning, collect three days of data on the number of words read correctly and the number of errors made in one minute reading timings.

Student Training:

1. Assign and teach various group roles to the students.

2. Develop and teach routines for moving into groups, distributing materials, getting help, and working when finished early.

3. Discuss and role-play certain social skills needed when working in groups.

4. Develop group goals and write them on the board.

5. Develop a product or assignment that the students need to show you that will reflect the amount of learning that took place during group time.

6. Plan a strategy for off-task behavior. For example, students will earn points for on-task behavior when the teacher periodically checks for good workers.

Treatment Procedure:

1. In elementary schools, an ideal time for peer tutoring would be when the teacher is working with the middle group of readers. At this time, a more fluent reader may be paired with two less fluent readers to practice.

2. The less fluent students can each practice reading a passage aloud two times.

3. As a student is reading, the more fluent peer may mark the number of words read incorrectly for the teacher.

4. The tutor can also correct any of the words that were read incorrectly or missed by simply telling the students the correct word.

5. When the less fluent student is called to his reading group to work with the teacher, the teacher can ask the student to read aloud for one minute. Assess the student's reading rate on the passage. Then tell the student that he will be reading as many words as he can within one minute. Set and start a timer for one minute. Tell the student to begin reading. If the student gets stuck on a word, tell the student the word after a 3 second delay. Mark any letter omitted or substituted as an error. Calculate the number of words the student said correctly.

6. The student may try to meet a goal of a certain number of words per minute or beat their best reading score with less than a certain number of errors. The teacher sets the goal. The teacher can give points or tokens to the tutor and student if the student's reading score improved.

7. As the teacher is working with the less fluent readers, the other reading groups may work on another assignment that is matched with their reading level. For example, the students can take turns reading out loud. Each group will then be required to complete an assignment based on the reading such as answering comprehension questions, practicing vocabulary or spelling, making predictions about the story, sequencing events, solving the problem, or writing a new ending.

Figure 35. Examples of Reading Errors

- **Word Substitution:**

  "dog" for "cat."

- **Mispronunciation:**

  "dig" for "dog."

- **Omits a word or a line of words.**

Progress Monitoring:

The number of words read correctly and the number of errors made in the one minute timed reading is to be recorded. The teacher can expect that the student's reading rate should consistently increase after five sessions in a row. Ideally, a student's number of errors will decrease to 1 or 2 mistakes while words correct will steadily increase (i.e., 60 words for 1st to 2nd grade and 100 for > than 3rd grade per minute).

Source:

Stevens, R.J., Madden, N.A., Slavin, R.E., & Farnish, A.M. (1987). Cooperative integrated reading and composition: Two field experiments. *Reading Research Quarterly, 22*, 433-454.

PEER TUTORS RECORD SHEET

Name ____________________

	Words Read		Errors	
	# Correct	Goal	# Incorrect	Goal
Monday				
Tuesday				
Wednesday				
Thursday				
Friday				

Increasing Reading Rate of Vocabulary Words Using Tape Recordings

Technique:

Many students are able to read words accurately but too slowly to comprehend the information presented in a passage. Reading rates increase the more the student is able to practice reading. However, the teacher may not be free to provide extra individual time for students who need extra practice to increase their reading rates. This intervention is designed to increase a student's reading rate while decreasing teacher attention time with the student.

Most Likely to Benefit:

Students who are able to read vocabulary sight words at a rate less than 40 words per minute often need additional practice sessions to increase the number of words they can read per minute.

Materials:

A list of vocabulary sight words, a timer, and a tape recording of the vocabulary words. A student or an adult can be taped reading the sight words at a fluent rate.

Baseline:

Assess the student's reading rate on vocabulary words. Tell the students that they will be reading as many words as they can within one minute. Set and start a timer for one minute. Tell the child to begin reading each of the words. If the student gets stuck on a word, tell the student the word after a 3-second delay. Mark any letter omitted or substituted as an error. Calculate the number of words the student read correctly.

Figure 36. Examples of Reading Errors

- **Word Substitution:**

  "dog" for "cat."

- **Mispronunciation:**

  "dig" for "dog."

- **Omits a word or a line of words.**

Treatment Procedure:

1. Copy a skill sheet or develop a list of 80 vocabulary words on paper.

2. Read the words in the order that they are written into a tape recorder at approximately 80 words per minute.

3. Instruct the student to practice reading the words along with the tape during a designated time each day. Some convenient times may be during center time, first thing in the morning, or during the last 10 minutes of the day.

4. Tell the student to read the words out loud without skipping any words. When the student is uncertain of the word, encourage the student to try to do their best.

5. Ask the student to read the words for one minute after the student has practiced reading with the tape recording.

6. Each word that is read correctly within three seconds will be marked as correct. If the student reads a word incorrectly, correct the student. If the student is stuck on a word, wait three seconds and then tell the student the word.

7. Record the number of words read correctly on the student's chart. Students often have fun trying to beat their best score.

Optional:

1. Many reading books used in the classroom are supplemented with tape recordings of each of the stories. These tapes may also be used to help increase a student's fluency in the same manner that was presented with vocabulary words.

2. Groups of two to three students may also read aloud with the tape together.

3. A peer can also be taught to mark words that are read incorrectly with the tape. After the tape session, the teacher can correct the student who missed words and have the student repeat the word(s) correctly.

Progress Monitoring:

By filling out a daily chart or graph, the teacher or student can keep track of the student progress and observe the student's daily improvement. The teacher can expect the student to increase the number of words read correctly to 70+ words per minute with a maximum of two errors before practicing another list of 80 vocabulary words.

Source:

Freeman, T.J. & McLaughlin, T.F. (1984). Effects of a taped-words treatment procedure on Learning Disabled Students' sight-word oral reading. *Learning Disability Quarterly*, 7, 49-53.

VOCABULARY RECORD SHEET

Student:____

List:____

Goal: Reading _____ words per minute with less than 2 errors.

Date	Words Read Correctly	Number of Errors

Cover, Copy, and Compare Math Procedure

Technique:

Many students need additional cues and practice before completing math problems correctly. In this procedure, the student first looks at how a problem is solved, then practices using the steps needed to do the problem correctly. Hence, students are provided with immediate corrective feedback and many additional opportunities to practice math facts and concepts. This procedure also promotes mastery with math problems without the use of peer tutors, additional teacher time, or additional materials.

Most Likely to Benefit:

Students who are having difficulty learning the necessary steps in computational problems may need additional practice and more specific feedback. If a student is performing below criteria (i.e., 20 digits per minute for 1st through 3rd grade or 30 digits per minute for 4th grade or higher), he or she may benefit from the additional practice and cues provided in this procedure.

Materials:

A math assignment, and a copy of the answers or another student's 100% correct paper.

Baseline:

Collect the student's previous class work and calculate the percentage of correct answers. If class work is unavailable, begin collecting class work in a folder.

Treatment Procedure:

1. This technique may be used before or after the student attempts to do the work independently. It can be used to monitor the student's work during independent seat work to check if the student is able to do the first few problems correctly. Or, use this procedure at the start of seat work if the student is consistently below 70% correct on class work.

2. Give the student a copy of the answers or another student's assignment that is neatly written, demonstrates the needed steps, and is 100% correct.

3. Tell the student to do the following five steps when working on each problem.

    a. Look at how the problem was solved.

    b. Cover the correct answer.

    c. Do the problem on your own paper.

    d. Uncover the correct answer.

    e. Compare your answer with the correct answer.

4. If needed, set a time limit for this procedure.

5. Once the student has finished the worksheet, give the student several problems that are similar to the problems practiced for two minutes. Tell the student to do them without using the cover, copy, and compare procedure.

6. If the student is able to do the additional few problems correctly, praise the student's work and provide a few minutes of free time. Or, the student may earn a decrease in the number of problems on his next homework assignment. If the student does not get all the problems correct, he or she can redo the cover, copy, and compare method. The teacher and student may also set a goal if the student is unable to get all the problems correct.

Progress Monitoring:

Evaluate the student progress on both the problems given after the cover, copy, and compare procedure and any independent seat work or homework given to the student using the same math skill. The student should be able to do most of the work correctly immediately after using this procedure. Moreover, the student's fluency (i.e., digits per minute) should increase when given the same types of problems during a timed assessment.

Source:

Skinner, C., Turco, T., Beatty, V., & Rasauage, C. (1989). Cover, copy, compare: A method for increasing multiplication fluency in behavior disordered children. *School Psychology Review*, *18*, 412-420.

COVER, COPY, COMPARE RECORD SHEET

Name: ______________________________

1. Look at how a problem was solved.
2. Cover the correct answer.
3. Do the problem on your own paper.
4. Uncover the correct answer.
5. Compare your answer with the correct answer.

Date	Percent Correct on Independent Problems	Did You Meet Your Goal?

Peer Tutoring in Math

Technique:

This procedure is designed to increase student accuracy and rate on basic math facts that are needed for more advanced computational problems. Moreover, this procedure allows teachers to monitor students' progress while students are busy providing each other with additional opportunities to practice math facts with immediate feedback.

Most Likely to Benefit:

Students who are performing below 20 digits correct per minute on basic math fact problems will benefit by increasing both their accuracy and fluency using this procedure.

Materials:

Math problems written on index cards with the answers written on the backs of the cards, student folders, skill sheet for testing, a timer, and student charts.

Baseline:

Give the students several skill sheets on basic facts. Tell the students to try to get as many problems correct as they can within two minutes. Use the skill sheets for the peer tutoring sessions that were scored at 20 digits or below.

Treatment Procedure:

1. Write the basic math facts on index cards. Each card should have the problem written on one side and the answer written on the other side. Students can make their own cards and keep them in their own folder.

2. Have the students work in pairs with each student working on 20-30 cards that match the problems presented on the skill sheets that they will be tested on.

3. The students or the teacher will set a timer for three minutes.

4. One student will present a card while the other student tries to say the correct answer.

5. If the student is unable to say the answer within five seconds, the student presenting the card will read the answer written on the back of the card.

6. When the timer goes off, the students will switch roles. The timer will be reset for another three minutes.

7. After the tutoring session, the teacher can assess both students on basic math skill sheets.

8. The teacher will set the timer and tell the students to start. The students will complete as many problems as they can within the two minutes.

9. Score the skill sheet by counting all of the correct digits. For example, $6 \times 6 = 30$ would count as one digit correct, whereas $6 \times 6 = 36$ would count as two digits correct.

10. Praise the students for correct answers. Moreover, students will earn a point each time that they are able to beat their best score on the same basic math skill sheet. In addition, the students get a point if both of them are able to beat their best scores. When the student pair collects a certain number of points and each person has at least a certain number of points, the student pair earns five minutes of activity time. The number of points should be adjusted such that the students are able to get activity time about every three days. In addition, students should be beating their best scores almost every day.

11. Remind the students to fill out their charts daily. Remember to cross off any points that have already been turned in for activity time.

Optional:

While the student is working on learning basic math facts, the student may also be able to work on learning steps for more advanced computational skills, allowing the student to use a calculator or a fact sheet with answers to problems, such as subtraction from 0 to 18. For example, the student can still learn subtraction with regrouping with the class while working on basic subtraction facts during peer tutoring sessions. This helps students to continue learning higher hierarchical skills with the class and prevents falling further behind their classmates.

Progress Monitoring:

A chart will be completed after each student's two-minute assessment. The student's progress in the number of digits correct in two minutes will be evaluated. The teacher can expect that the student will be working toward 100-140 digits correct within two minutes. When the student has mastered the skill sheet at this rate, give the student an additional sheet and change the problems on their index cards to match the skill tested on the new skill sheet.

When monitoring a student pair's progress, several factors may need to be readjusted to increase the effectiveness of this procedure. First, the students' cards may be too difficult if the students are not beating their best scores. In this case, reduce the cards to only 10 per tutoring session. Or, if the students are answering their problems too quickly, then add more challenging problems during the tutoring session. Moreover, the problems may be too simple if they are correctly completing close to 140 digits per minute. Also, the students may not be presenting the cards quickly to each other. If this is this case, shorten the amount of time they are given to present the cards and show the students how to present each card quickly and provide assistance within three seconds. Finally, the students may not be earning enough points to get their activity time. This may be a result of the peer tutors not adequately giving error corrections to each other. The teacher can monitor several tutoring sessions closely and prompt students to correct each other as needed. If needed, the peer tutors can get points for presenting the cards quickly and giving the answers quickly to each other during a tutoring session.

Sources:

Heron, T.E., Heward, W.L., Cooke, N.L., & Hill, D.S. (1993). Evaluation of a classwide peer tutoring system: First graders teach each other words. *Education and Treatment of Children, 14*, 216-228.

Greenwood, C.R., Terry, B., Arreaga-Mayer, C., & Finney, R. (1992). The classwide peer tutoring program: Implementation factors moderating students' achievement. *Journal of Applied Behavior, 25*, 101-116.

Horton, S., Lovitt, T., & White, O. (1992). Teaching mathematics to adolescents classified as educable mentally handicapped: Using calculators to remove computational onus. *Journal of Remedial and Special Education, 13*, 36-60.

MATH RECORD SHEET FOR PEER TUTORING

Name: ______________________________

Date	Digits Correct per 2 minutes	Best Score	Points for Beating Your Score	Activity Earned

Cuing Students' Spelling Errors

Technique: This is a simple procedure that promotes spelling accuracy on weekly spelling tests by cuing students on the parts of words that are misspelled.

Most Likely to Benefit: This procedure is most helpful for students who are consistently getting below 70% correct on weekly spelling tests but who are reading above 40 words per minute on grade level.

Materials: Weekly spelling words.

Baseline: Collect the results of the last five weekly spelling tests.

Treatment Procedure: While teaching the weekly spelling lesson as usual, include the following steps throughout the week.

Monday

1. Give students a list of spelling words.
2. Say the words aloud for the students.
3. Tell the students to study the words on their own.

Tuesday

4. Give the students a pretest by saying each of the words aloud to the students.
5. Grade the test.
6. Circle the misspelled part of each word with red ink to highlight the type of errors made.
7. Tell the students to write the correct words next to the misspelled word.

Friday

8. Give the final spelling test to assess for spelling accuracy.

Progress Monitoring:

Place the pretests and spelling tests for each student in a folder. At the end of each session, have the student record the number of errors made on each test. The teacher can expect an improvement in the student's performance on the Friday test. If, however, the student's scores are not consistently 85% or above, the student may need additional practice writing the spelling words. A more intensive approach is used in the Write/Say method.

Source:

Gettinger, M. (1995). Effects of teacher-directed versus student-directed instruction and cues versus no cues for improving spelling performance. *Journal of Applied Behavior Analysis, 18*, 167-171.

Add-A-Word Spelling Practice

Technique: Students who are having difficulty learning the weekly spelling words may need additional practice and more specific feedback. This procedure assists students in mastering spelling words without the use of peer tutors, additional teacher time, and additional materials. Yet students are provided with immediate corrective feedback and with additional opportunities to practice spelling words.

Most Likely to Benefit: This procedure is most helpful for students who are consistently getting below 70% correct on weekly spelling tests and who are reading below 40 words per minute on grade level.

Materials: A copy of the weekly spelling words and an "Add-A-Word" worksheet.

Baseline: Collect the results of the last five weekly spelling tests.

Treatment Procedure:

1. Tell the student to copy 10 spelling words to practice in the copy column.
2. Cover the words.
3. Tell the student to write the 10 words from memory.
4. Uncover the copied words.
5. Compare the responses with the correct spelling sheet.
6. Repeat this process at a later time. Some students may need to do this two times per day in order to learn all of the required weekly spelling words.
7. After two trials, keep any misspelled word on the list of 10 practice words.

8. Drop words that are spelled correctly after they are spelled correctly in two consecutive trials. Add a new word for every word that is dropped.

9. If all of the weekly spelling words are correct, then have the student practice all of the words again at one time.

10. If needed, set a time limit for this procedure.

11. Keep the Add-A-Word worksheets and the weekly spelling test in a folder.

12. The student should fill out a daily chart and keep it in his folder.

Progress Monitoring: Evaluate the student's progress on the weekly spelling test after the Add-A-Word procedure. The student scores should increase to 90% or above. If the student's scores are not increasing or words are not added on their practice sheet, begin giving bonus points for every word added and/or every word spelled correctly.

Source:

Pratt-Struthers, J., Struthers, J., and Williams, R. (1983). The effects of the add-a-word spelling program on spelling accuracy during creative writing. *Education and Treatment of Children, 6* (3), 277-283.

ADD-A-WORD

Name: ______________________________

Copy	Practice	If Correct Add a + If Incorrect Add a -
1.		
2.		
3.		
4.		
5.		
6.		
7.		
8.		
9.		
10.		

RECORD SHEET FOR ADD-A-WORD SPELLING

Name: ______________________________

Date	Number of Words Correct	Number of Words Added
Monday		
Tuesday		
Wednesday		
Thursday		
TEST		

Using Peer Editors for Writing

Technique:

Once students are writing fairly rapidly and in a way that is organized and makes sense, students often need to revise their work. However, students often do not know how to revise their work and teachers do not have the time to provide frequent and immediate feedback for the students. Hence, students can be taught how to look for mistakes in their writing and how to correct their mistakes. This procedure is designed to give students additional opportunity to revise their and other students' writing while receiving immediate feedback on their own papers.

Most Likely to Benefit:

Students who are writing at an adequate number of words per minute and their stories have a comprehensible structure to them but their work is often grammatically incorrect. This procedure will help students to revise their own writing, resulting in a decrease in grammar errors.

Materials:

Writing assignments.

Baseline:

Collect the last three writing assignments. Calculate the average number of errors made on the skills that are to be targeted in this intervention (e.g., the number of mistakes made with capitalization, punctuation, and grammar).

Treatment Procedure:

1. Use stories that the students have written in class. Begin with shorter stories. For example, have students each write a story for 10 minutes after first giving a story starter.

2. Tell the students that they will be helping each other correct their work.

3. Select several grammar errors that the students will look for in their papers. Students will need to be explicitly taught any mechanical writing error that they will be identifying and correcting.

4. Show some examples of the grammar errors and how students are to indicate errors on the papers they will be revising.

5. Demonstrate how the errors should be corrected.

6. Show students how their papers will be scored. For example, score one point for less than two capitalization errors, one point for less than two punctuation errors, and one point for less than two errors using "is" and "are" (see the Writing Score Sheet example).

7. List the rating sheets with the goals in visible areas.

8. Direct the students to write their stories. Give a time limit.

9. Allow students to first correct their own papers.

10. After revising their own papers, have students work in groups of two or three.

11. Students can exchange papers to check for needed revisions. If needed, set a timer each time the students switch stories.

12. Each student may receive points or bonus points for both her own final version of the story and her partner's final version.

Progress Monitoring:

The papers may be evaluated in several ways. For example, the number of words written and the number of mechanical errors may be monitored. The errors can be broken down into each step that is presented to the students, such as capitalization, periods, commas, or grammatical errors.

Sources:

Stoddard, B. & MacArthur, C.A. (1993). A peer editor strategy: Guiding learning-disabled students in response and revision. *Research in the Teaching of English*, *27*, 76-103.

Graham, S., MacArthur, C., Schwartz, S., & Page-Voth, V. (1992). Improving the compositions of students with learning disabilities using a strategy involving product and process goal setting. *Exceptional Children*, *41*, 322-334.

WRITING SCORE SHEET

Name: ______________________________

Skill	Goal
1.	☐ point(s) for less than ☐ errors.
2.	☐ point(s) for less than ☐ errors.
3.	☐ point(s) for less than ☐ errors.
4.	☐ point(s) for less than ☐ errors.
5.	☐ point(s) for less than ☐ errors.
6.	☐ point(s) for less than ☐ errors.

Decreasing Spelling Errors in Writing

Technique: Students often make a number of spelling errors when incorporating vocabulary words into their writing. This procedure provides teachers with a simple way to help students overcome spelling difficulties as they write on specific topics.

Most Likely to Benefit: This procedure will assist students who are misspelling approximately 30% of the words written.

Materials: A writing topic, a sheet of poster board or overhead transparency, and a dictionary.

Baseline: Collect the last three writing assignments that the student wrote in class. Calculate how many spelling errors were made on the last three writing assignments per number of words written.

Treatment Procedure:

1. Present a writing topic to the students.
2. Brainstorm ideas with the class that may be included in the students' papers or stories.
3. Generate vocabulary words that may be used when writing on a specific topic.
4. Write the words on the chalk board, overhead, or poster board.
5. Post the words in a visible area while students are writing on the topic.
6. Allow students to use a dictionary when needed.
7. Provide a peer helper for students who may need additional help when looking up words in the dictionary.

8. See the peer editing intervention strategy for further assistance in decreasing spelling errors.

Progress Monitoring: The number of spelling errors made per number of written words should decrease with the use of posted vocabulary words, a dictionary, and peer assistance.

Problem Solving: If a student's number of spelling errors is not decreasing as expected, try to reinforce the student for using the posted vocabulary words or dictionary. Simply tell the student to underline the vocabulary word or to write the page number that the word was found on in the dictionary next to the word.

Praise the student and/or give bonus points for a certain number of correctly spelled words that are underlined or have a page number beside them.

Source:

Gleason, M. & Issacson, S. (1991). The effect of four types of teacher spelling assistance on the written expression of mildly handicapped children. *The Oregon Monograph Conference 1991*. Eugene: Division on Teacher Education and Rehabilitation, University of Oregon.

SPELLING RECORD SHEET

Student: ____

Date	Number of Words	Number of Spelling Errors	Errors/ Words	Number of Words Underlined or With Page #	Goal

APPENDIX

Basic Skill Builders Skill Sheet Bank

Available from Sopris West (800) 547-6747

Skill	Number of Sheets
Math	
Addition	63
Subtraction	41
Multiplication	60
Division	24
Math Tool Skills	61
Count Bys	44
Story Problems	52
Metric Units	65
Roman Numerals	31
Complex Addition	28
Complex Subtraction	13
Fractions	46
Decimals	30
Grammar	
Nouns	13
Pronouns	3
Verbs	37
Articles	1
Adjectives	18
Adverbs	13
Prepositions	4
Conjunctions	6
Interjections	1

Skill	Number of Sheets
Grammar (cont'd)	
Sentence Structure	50
Punctuation	43
Capitalization	17
Vocabulary Development	19
Dictionary Skills	31
Reading	
Kindergarten Pinpoints	18
Phonics	58
Beginning Reading	28
Reading Skills	118
Other	
Spelling	90
Handwriting	120
Telling Time	40
Map Skills	44
Money	15

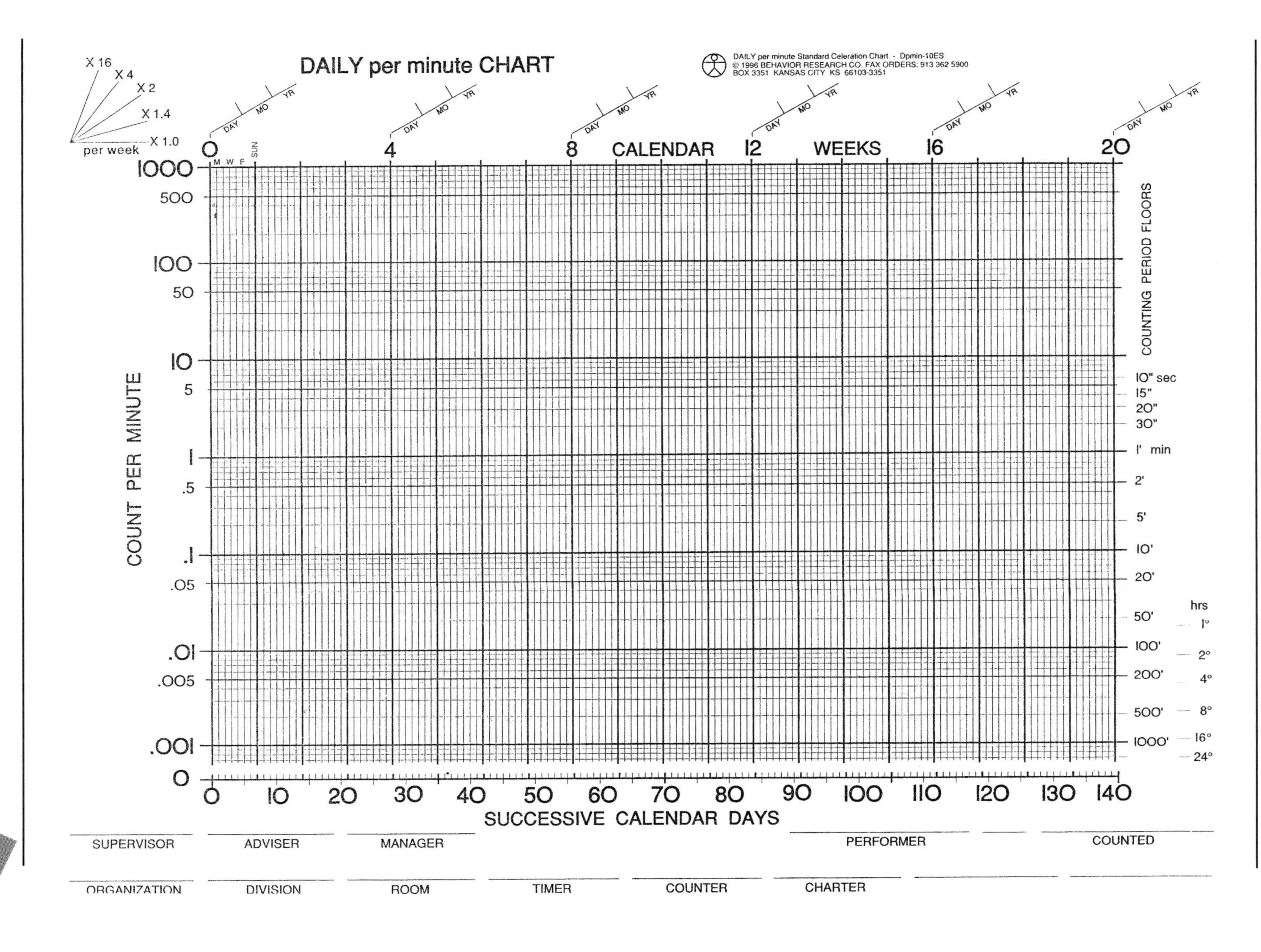
DAILY per minute CHART
DAILY per minute Standard Celeration Chart - Dpmin-10ES
© 1996 BEHAVIOR RESEARCH CO. FAX ORDERS: 913 362 5900
BOX 3351 KANSAS CITY KS 66103-3351
X 16
X 4
X 2
X 1.4
X 1.0
per week
DAY MO YR
0 4 8 CALENDAR 12 WEEKS 16 20
M W F SUN
COUNT PER MINUTE
1000 500 100 50 10 5 1 .5 .1 .05 .01 .005 .001 0
COUNTING PERIOD FLOORS
10" sec 15" 20" 30" 1' min 2' 5' 10' 20' 50' 100' 200' 500' 1000'
hrs 1° 2° 4° 8° 16° 24°
0 10 20 30 40 50 60 70 80 90 100 110 120 130 140
SUCCESSIVE CALENDAR DAYS
SUPERVISOR
ADVISER
MANAGER
PERFORMER
COUNTED
ORGANIZATION
DIVISION
ROOM
TIMER
COUNTER
CHARTER

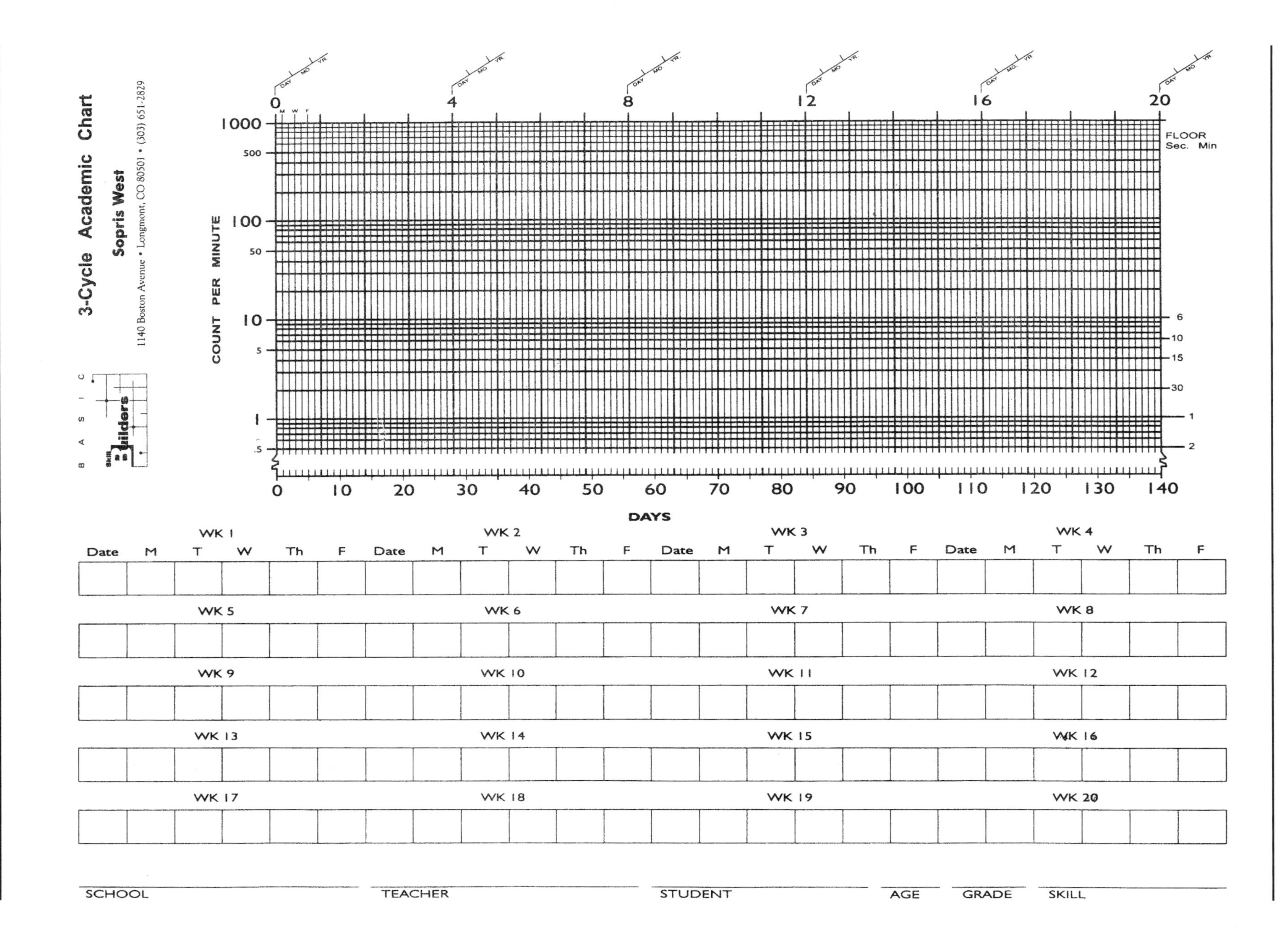
3-Cycle Academic Chart
Sopris West
1140 Boston Avenue • Longmont, CO 80501 • (303) 651-2829
Skill Builders
BASIC
COUNT PER MINUTE
DAYS
FLOOR
Sec. Min
WK 1
WK 2
WK 3
WK 4
Date M T W Th F
WK 5
WK 6
WK 7
WK 8
WK 9
WK 10
WK 11
WK 12
WK 13
WK 14
WK 15
WK 16
WK 17
WK 18
WK 19
WK 20
SCHOOL
TEACHER
STUDENT
AGE
GRADE
SKILL

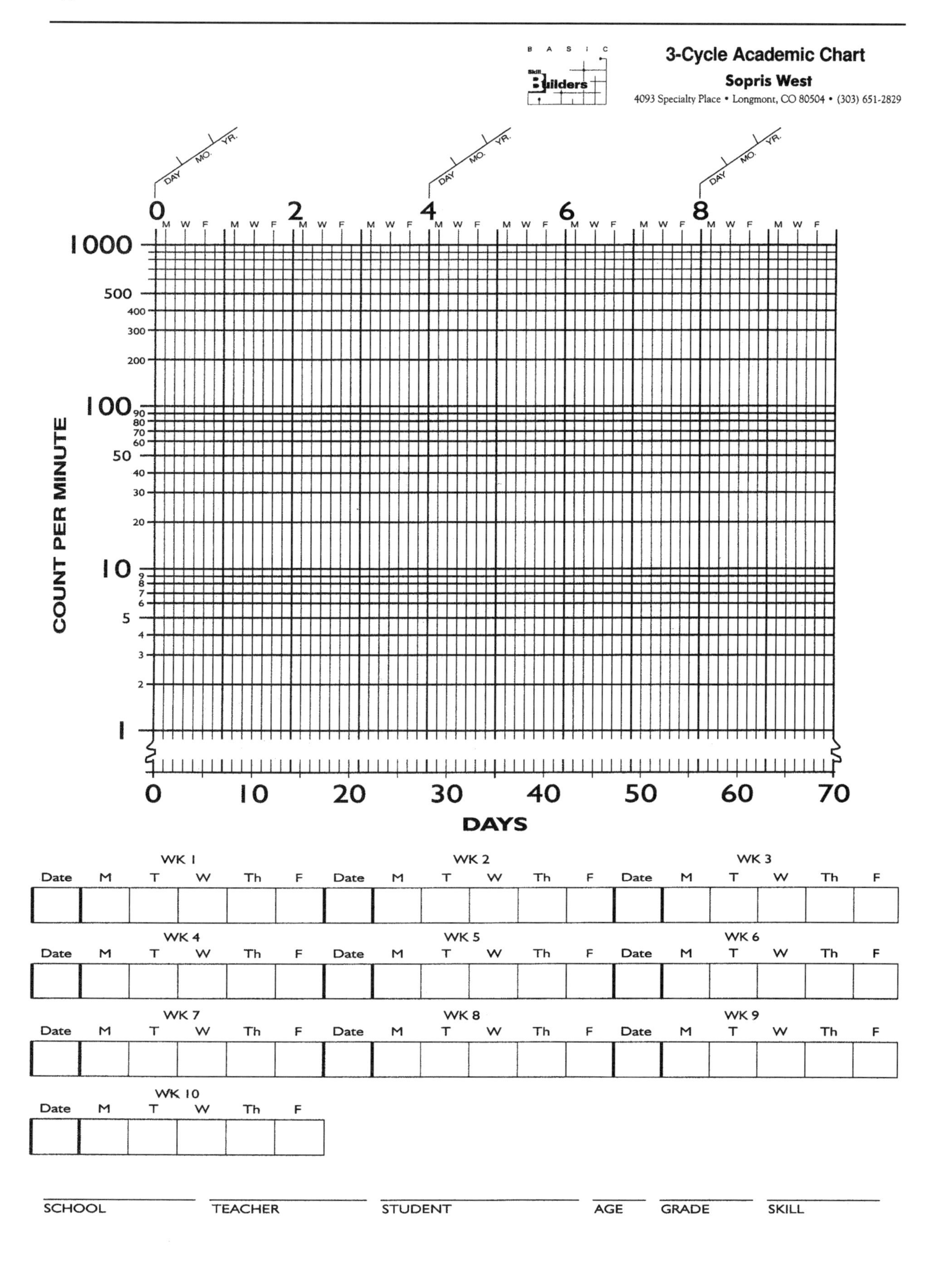
BASIC Skill Builders
3-Cycle Academic Chart
Sopris West
4093 Specialty Place • Longmont, CO 80504 • (303) 651-2829
DAY
MO.
YR.
0
2
4
6
8
M W F
1000
500
400
300
200
100
90
80
70
60
50
40
30
20
10
9
8
7
6
5
4
3
2
1
COUNT PER MINUTE
0
10
20
30
40
50
60
70
DAYS
WK 1
WK 2
WK 3
WK 4
WK 5
WK 6
WK 7
WK 8
WK 9
WK 10
Date
M
T
W
Th
F
SCHOOL
TEACHER
STUDENT
AGE
GRADE
SKILL

SEE TO WRITE

	Correct	Error
First Try		
Second Try		

Multiplication: Triple Digit Times Triple Digit Without Regrouping

113 x 221	310 x 533	222 x 222	200 x 514	122 x 244	(74)
222 x 222	122 x 244	310 x 533	113 x 221	200 x 514	(148)
122 x 244	200 x 514	222 x 222	310 x 533	113 x 221	(222)

SEE TO WRITE

	Correct	Error
First Try		
Second Try		

2 Digit Divisor Without Remainder in the Answer

50)2000	17)442	27)1566	49)2744	51)1632	38)1406	(60)
49)2744	27)1566	17)442	51)1632	50)2000	38)1406	(120)
50)2000	38)1406	51)1632	49)2744	27)1566	17)442	(180)
51)1632	50)2000	27)1566	17)442	49)2744	38)1406	(240)

SEE TO WRITE

	Correct	Error
First Try		
Second Try		

Writing—Cursive i

i i i i i i i i i

i i i i i i i i i

i i i i i i i i i

i

i

SEE TO SAY

	Correct	Error
First Try		
Second Try		

Sound Symbols—ing Words

Directions: Say each word.

sing	wing	ring	king	bring	dink	fling	sing	wing	ring	(10)
sling	cling	fling	sting	swing	singing	winging	sling	cling	fling	(20)
ringing	bringing	dinging	paying	wishing	farming	chaining	ringing	bringing	dinging	(30)
beating	fishing	kicking	backing	packing	cheering	hushing	beating	fishing	kicking	(40)
matching	morning	arming	arming	slinging	parking	pitching	matching	morning	arming	(50)
catching	racking	harming	sorting	saying	slaying	marching	catching	racking	harming	(60)
playing	raining	holding	shocking	gaining	barking	laying	playing	raining	holding	(70)
feeding	bringing	howling	boating	shouting	licking	waiting	feeding	bringing	howling	(80)
steaming	howling	mocking	charming	hushing	farming	staying	steaming	howling	mocking	(90)
dreaming	laying	shouting	gaining	barking	holding	scolding	dreaming	laying	shouting	(100)
ring	cling	sting	wing	king	fling	bring	ring	cling	string	(110)
marching	matching	harming	feeling	darting	licking	boating	marching	matching	harming	(120)

SEE TO SAY

	Correct	Error
First Try		
Second Try		

Passages—Pre-Primer Level #1

Directions: Say each word.

My house is down here. Will you come down to my house and play with me? I want (18)
you to come and see my little red ball. You will see my big blue ball. We will jump (37)
up and down. We will make the big blue ball jump up and down. The little ball is (55)
not blue. It is red. We will not make it jump up and down. You will play with the (74)
big blue ball and I will play with the little red ball. My father said to me, "Mother and I (94)
will come to get you. We will come for you in a big red car. We will not come for you (115)
in a little blue car." My mother said to me, "Oh! The car is not little and it is not blue. (136)
We will come for you in a big red car." Oh! Here is my father. See the car. Look! Oh, (156)
see! It is a red car. Jump in and ride. Ride to my house. (170)

SEE TO WRITE

	Correct	Error
First Try		
Second Try		

Telling Time (5 minutes after the hour)

Directions: Draw the hands on the clock for the given time.

12:05 6:05 3:05 8:05 (8)

10:05 7:05 2:05 9:05 (16)

1:05 4:05 11:05 10:05 (24)

	Correct	Error
First Try		
Second Try		

SEE TO WRITE

Adverbs

Directions: After each sentence, write what the underlined adverb tells: Where? When? How? or To What Extent?

Come here, Fred.	________	Sometimes Jill plays golf with her dad.	________	(2)
Greg makes too many excuses.	________	She drove carefully.	________	(4)
He is leaving the store now.	________	Alice spoke softly but distinctly.	________	(6)
I will meet you there.	________	Joe was extremely late.	________	(8)
We should turn right.	________	Shelley looked around.	________	(10)
He rises early.	________	He was stealing cautiously along the wall.	________	(12)
He receives his paycheck monthly.	________	This hat is too big.	________	(14)
They ate their lunch quickly.	________	The principal will be here soon.	________	(16)
The library will be open tomorrow.	________	The students talked quietly for an hour.	________	(18)
The Indians silently took their places.	________	Tonight I will grade your papers.	________	(20)
He reads the paper daily.	________	The building is especially high.	________	(22)
Haven't you ever wanted to go there?	________	Occasionally he forgets his homework.	________	(24)
The players left the field quickly.	________	She slowly raised the rifle and fired.	________	(26)
The door banged and in walked the teacher.	________	The Mohicans boldly sent back the enemy.	________	(28)
Mrs. Leatham types fast.	________	They arrived at the party late.	________	(30)
The new student is never on time.	________	Please put the books down.	________	(32)
She reacted very calmly.	________	The stereo was playing softly.	________	(34)
We'll be home tomorrow.	________	The little girl looked sadly at the doll.	________	(36)

Sample Packet—Page 63

	Correct	Error
First Try		
Second Try		

SEE TO WRITE

Decimals—Add Money

$3.83 + 3.57	$2.48 + 1.86	$3.47 + 1.03	$6.48 + 1.24	$3.73 + 1.76	$6.55 + 1.44	$6.55 + 2.02	$8.59 + 2.63	
$7.40	$4.34	$4.50	$7.72	$5.49	$7.99	$8.57	$11.22	
$2.48 + 1.86	$6.48 + 1.24	$3.73 + 1.76	$6.65 + 2.02	$2.48 + 1.86	$3.83 + 3.57	$6.55 + 1.44	$6.65 + 2.02	(24)
$3.47 + 1.03	$6.48 + 1.24	$3.73 + 1.76	$6.65 + 2.02	$6.55 + 1.44	$2.48 + 1.86	$3.73 + 1.76	$8.59 + 2.63	(49)
$2.48 + 1.86	$3.47 + 1.03	$3.73 + 1.76	$6.55 + 1.44	$8.59 + 2.63	$3.47 + 1.03	$2.48 + 1.86	$3.83 + 3.57	(74)
$2.48 + 1.86	$3.47 + 1.03	$3.73 + 1.76	$6.55 + 1.44	$6.55 + 2.02	8.59 + 2.63	$3.73 + 1.76	$2.48 + 1.86	(99)
$3.83 + 3.57	$2.48 + 1.86	$3.47 + 1.03	$6.48 + 1.24	$3.73 + 1.76	$6.55 + 1.44	$6.44 + 2.02	$3.47 + 1.03	(123)

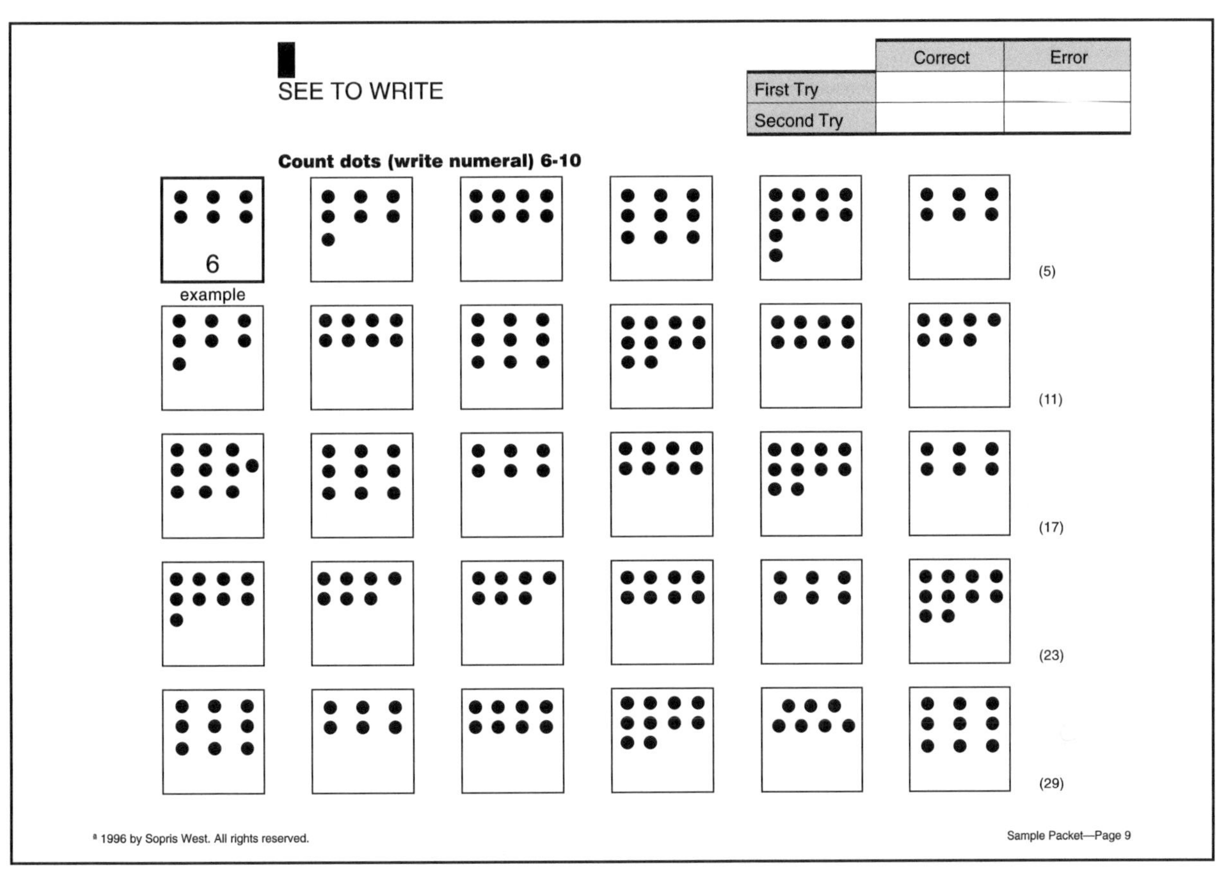

SEE TO WRITE

	Correct	Error
First Try		
Second Try		

Count dots (write numeral) 6-10

6

example

(5)

(11)

(17)

(23)

(29)

Sample Packet—Page 9

SEE TO WRITE

	Correct	Error
First Try		
Second Try		

Common and Proper Nouns

Directions: Mark (P) for proper noun and (C) for common noun.

tree _____	forest _____	basketball _____	Russia _____	child _____	(5)
California _____	Water Avenue _____	Salt Lake City _____	donkey _____	car _____	(10)
Utah _____	Spanish _____	English _____	Scotland _____	country _____	(15)
Pacific Ocean _____	river _____	Oldsmobile _____	car _____	Pontiac _____	(20)
George Smith _____	Gulf of Mexico _____	Abraham Lincoln ___	ocean _____	mother _____	(25)
mountain _____	Mount Rainier _____	star _____	Star Wars _____	secretary _____	(30)
state _____	Monday _____	September _____	Mexico _____	Christmas _____	(35)
library _____	Indian _____	men _____	Robin Hood _____	mouse _____	(40)
prairie _____	Texas _____	fog _____	Jordan River _____	hill _____	(45)
Lincoln Jr. High _____	school _____	Jefferson School Dist. ___	aunt _____	uncle _____	(50)
Doctor Strangelove ___	kitten _____	book _____	Uncle Remus ____	window _____	(55)
The Bible _____	bible _____	Webster's Dictionary ____	Donny Osmond ___	arithmetic _____	(60)
encyclopedia _____	New York City _____	Wyoming _____	Tuesday _____	January _____	(65)

Sample Packet—Page 55

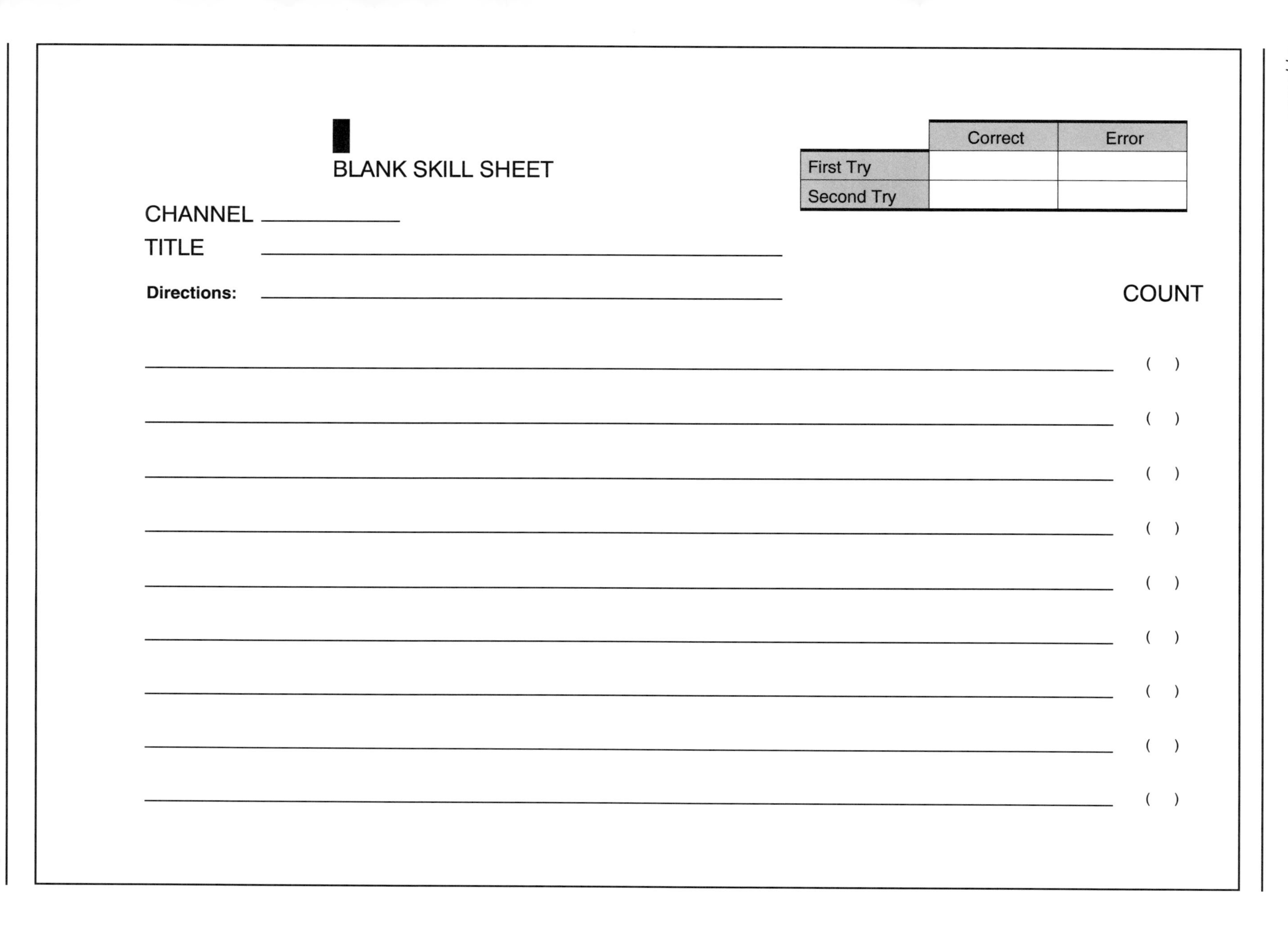

BLANK SKILL SHEET

	Correct	Error
First Try		
Second Try		

CHANNEL ______

TITLE ______

Directions: ______

COUNT

______ ( )

______ ( )

______ ( )

______ ( )

______ ( )

______ ( )

______ ( )

______ ( )

______ ( )

MORE SOPRIS WEST RESOURCES

Basic Skill Builders

Helping students become fluent in basic skills

Ray Beck, Ed.D.; Denise Conrad, Ed.D.; and Peggy Anderson, Ph.D.

Grades: K-12

This special and regular education program builds and maintains fluency (accuracy plus speed) in basic skills. It meets the needs of students who require additional practice. Nearly 1,500 *Skill Builder Sheets* linked with one-minute practice exercises enable students to practice skills, see their own progress, and self-monitor accuracy. Sets are available for math, language, reading, and spelling. 50 *Basic Skill Packets* are also available for such skill areas as map skills, telling time, and handwriting. The 88-page *Handbook* helps teachers or parents implement the program successfully. The *Student Materials Kit* contains items sufficient for 30 students, including folders, pens, acetates, charts, and sponges.

Clear objectives and meaningful feedback result in immediate, positive changes in achievement. This program, formerly *Precision Teaching*, uses principles of precision teaching to improve students' ability to remember, transfer to more complex tasks, and apply the skill to everyday life.

Conducting Functional Behavioral Assessments

A Practical Guide

Ron Nelson, Ph.D.; Maura Roberts, Ph.D.; and Deborah Smith, Ph.D.

Grades: K-12

Meet IDEA '97 requirements for conducting functional behavioral assessments (FBAs) with this practical guide and accompanying data collection forms. When standard classroom management strategies are not working effectively, Conducting Functional Behavioral Assessments provides step-by-step procedures for gathering pertinent behavioral information. Guiding principles help you develop a behavioral intervention plan that matches interventions and supports to the function(s) of targeted behaviors. Examples of common classroom scenarios illustrate how to determine the specific antecedents and consequences that occur around target behaviors. Useful background information on FBAs is offered, including why FBAs should be conducted and when they are necessary under IDEA '97. 49 pages.

Four easy-to-use Data Collection Forms (Interview/Self Report; Observation and Analysis; Temporal Analysis and Ranking; and Summary Analysis) help you collect and organize your data into a useable format for developing appropriate behavioral plans.

C112SET Conducting Functional Behavioral Assessements with set of four forms (10 of each)

C112FORMS Complete set of four forms (10 of each)

TGIF: But What Will I Do on Monday?

Susan L. Fister, M.Ed. and Karen A. Kemp, M.A.

Grades: 1-12

These 175 effective, instructional modification procedures for accommodating students will help you overcome instructional challenges and fully engage your students in learning. Simply look up the specific challenge faced and select from a list of research-based solutions in four key areas: teacher-directed instruction, guided practice activities, independent practice activities, and final measurement. TGIF provides proven strategies for getting your students to:

- Achieve classroom goals and objectives
- Remember and utilize information
- Respond to instructions
- Get organized
- Perform better on tests
- And more

178 pages. Implementing these strategies is even easier with TGIF: Making It Work on Monday, the companion book of reproducibles.

TGIF: Making It Work on Monday

These 100 reproducible masters for teachers and students make instructional accommodation even easier. Includes tracking sheets, organizing forms, handouts, activity sheets, and more. 204 pages. Training Available

C61SET Set: TGIF: But What Will I Do on Monday? and Making It Work Best Value!

C61TG TGIF: But What Will I Do on Monday?

C61CP TGIF: Making It Work

Call for more information about these and other Sopris West resources.

(800) 547-6747